LISTENING WITH SPEAKING

牛津技能世界
英语听说专项训练 2

［英］萨拉·简·刘易斯-曼察里斯◎著　　石若琳◎译

北京科学技术出版社
100 层 童 书 馆

图书在版编目（CIP）数据

牛津技能世界. 英语听说专项训练 2 /（英）萨拉·简·刘易斯－曼察里斯著；石若琳译. -- 北京：北京科学技术出版社，2025. -- ISBN 978-7-5714-4474-7

Ⅰ. G624.313

中国国家版本馆 CIP 数据核字第 2025RC8330 号

策划编辑：闫　娉
责任编辑：樊川燕
封面设计：包荧莹
图文制作：史维肖
责任印制：吕　越
出 版 人：曾庆宇
出版发行：北京科学技术出版社
社　　址：北京西直门南大街16号
邮政编码：100035
ISBN 978-7-5714-4474-7

电　　话：0086-10-66135495（总编室）
　　　　　0086-10-66113227（发行部）
网　　址：www.bkydw.cn
印　　刷：雅迪云印（天津）科技有限公司
开　　本：889 mm × 1194 mm　1/16
字　　数：165千字
印　　张：8.25
版　　次：2025年3月第1版
印　　次：2025年3月第1次印刷

定　　价：91.50元

Table of Contents

Introduction

“牛津技能世界：英语听说专项训练”系列将英语听力和英语口语的学习以灵活有趣的方式结合到一起，着眼于策略和技巧的教授，有助于学生自主学习并达成学习目标。

快来开启你的探险之旅吧!

大家好，我们是奥利和莫莉，也是牛津技能世界探险之旅的向导。我们会讲授实用的听力和口语学习策略，提出有针对性的问题并给出合理的建议，帮助你达成学习目标。相信在我们的陪伴下，你的探险之旅将充满乐趣！还在等什么？快开始吧！

Quick Guide

引入话题

话题贴近学生生活，且都基于特定的主题。

这里列出了每个单元*的学习目标。

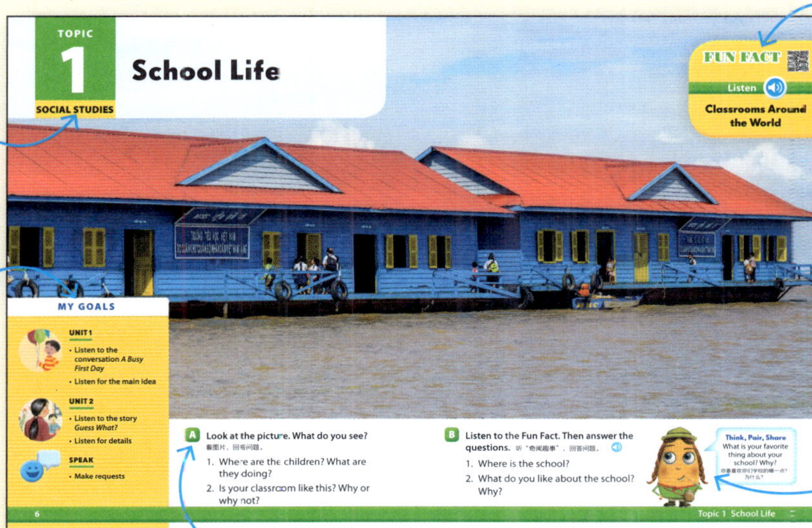

奇闻趣事
旨在快速激发学生的学习兴趣。

奥利和莫莉会引导学生进行思考、合作与交流。

设置问题，激活学生的背景知识，引导学生进行思辨。

听前准备和听力训练

学生学习重点词汇，并在本书后面的“图解词典”中写出相应的单词或短语。

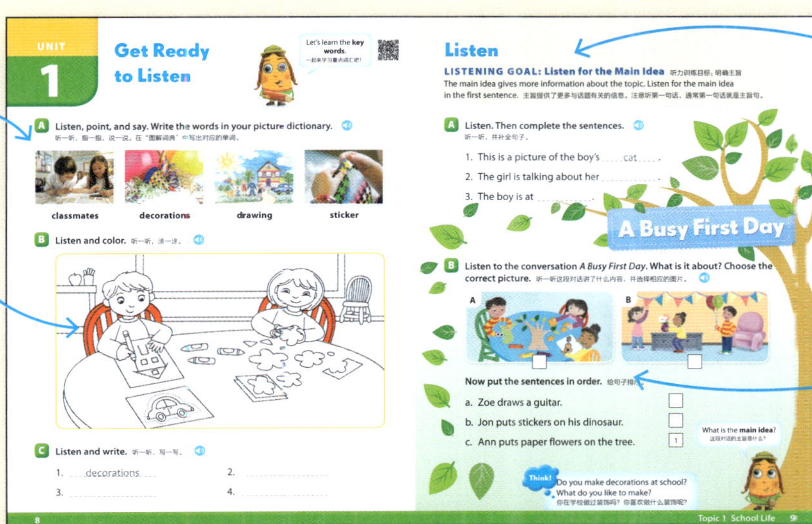

这里介绍了超级实用的听力学习策略。

听力学习策略能帮助学生应对不同类型的听力材料，不管是虚构类的还是非虚构类的。听录音的时候，学生应联系生活实际进行思辨。

* 每个话题包含两个主题相近的单元。

加深理解

引导学生运用听力学习策略来更好地理解听到的内容。

检验学生对本单元内容，包括词汇和语法的掌握程度。

设置相关练习，帮助学生进一步掌握所学词汇。

设置更多练习，帮助学生了解不同的题型，以更好地应对考试。

Understand

A Think about *A Busy First Day*. What is the main idea?

Remember! Listen for the **main idea** in the first sentence.

☐ a. The students are making a learning tree on the first day of school.

☐ b. The students are drawing pictures of a tree on the first day of school.

B Listen to *A Busy First Day* again. Choose the correct answer.

1. Zoe and Jon are **at home** / **at school**.
2. Ann's decorations are **flowers** / **flags**.
3. The decorations are **orange** / **pink**.
4. Jon makes a **dinosaur** / **flower**.
5. Zoe makes **a drawing** / **some stickers**.

C Listen. Complete each sentence with a key word. Then match.

1. They are my favorite classmates.
2. Those are our ________.
3. We have a lot of ________.
4. You can see my ________ on my desk.

a. ____ b. 1 c. ____ d. ____

D Listen to *A Busy First Day* again. Work with a partner. Complete the diagram.

decorations drawing pencil stickers

1. drawing 2. ________ 3. ________ 4. ________ (that / those)

E Look at **D**. Write. Use *that* or *those*.

1. Is that your drawing?
2. ________ are my friend's stickers.
3. ________ is my green pencil.
4. What are ________?

MY LISTENING GOALS

☐ I can listen to the conversation.

☐ I can listen for the main idea.

10 Topic 1 School Life 11

听力测试

奥利和莫莉会引导学生运用学到的听力学习策略。

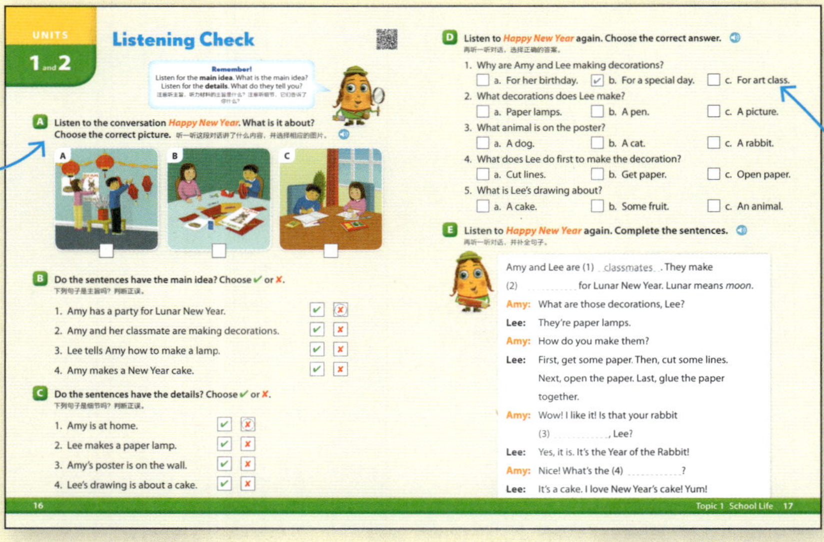

UNITS 1 and 2

Listening Check

Remember! Listen for the **main idea**. What is the main idea? Listen for the **details**. What do they tell you?

A Listen to the conversation *Happy New Year*. What is it about? Choose the correct picture.

A ☐ B ☐ C ☐

B Do the sentences have the main idea? Choose ✔ or ✘.

1. Amy has a party for Lunar New Year.
2. Amy and her classmate are making decorations.
3. Lee tells Amy how to make a lamp.
4. Amy makes a New Year cake.

C Do the sentences have the details? Choose ✔ or ✘.

1. Amy is at home.
2. Lee makes a paper lamp.
3. Amy's poster is on the wall.
4. Lee's drawing is about a cake.

D Listen to *Happy New Year* again. Choose the correct answer.

1. Why are Amy and Lee making decorations?
   ☐ a. For her birthday. ☑ b. For a special day. ☐ c. For art class.
2. What decorations does Lee make?
   ☐ a. Paper lamps. ☐ b. A pen. ☐ c. A picture.
3. What animal is on the poster?
   ☐ a. A dog. ☐ b. A cat. ☐ c. A rabbit.
4. What does Lee do first to make the decoration?
   ☐ a. Cut lines. ☐ b. Get paper. ☐ c. Open paper.
5. What is Lee's drawing about?
   ☐ a. A cake. ☐ b. Some fruit. ☐ c. An animal.

E Listen to *Happy New Year* again. Complete the sentences.

Amy and Lee are (1) classmates. They make (2) ________ for Lunar New Year. Lunar means *moon*.

Amy: What are those decorations, Lee?

Lee: They're paper lamps.

Amy: How do you make them?

Lee: First, get some paper. Then, cut some lines. Next, open the paper. Last, glue the paper together.

Amy: Wow! I like it! Is that your rabbit (3) ________, Lee?

Lee: Yes, it is. It's the Year of the Rabbit!

Amy: Nice! What's the (4) ________?

Lee: It's a cake. I love New Year's cake! Yum!

16 Topic 1 School Life 17

学生完成相关练习，进一步强化听力理解和词汇运用能力。

口语交际和说一说

口语训练目标
旨在帮助学生在不同的场景下自信表达。

口语练习小贴士
提供语法、标点符号和学习策略方面的指导，帮助学生准确、流利地交流。

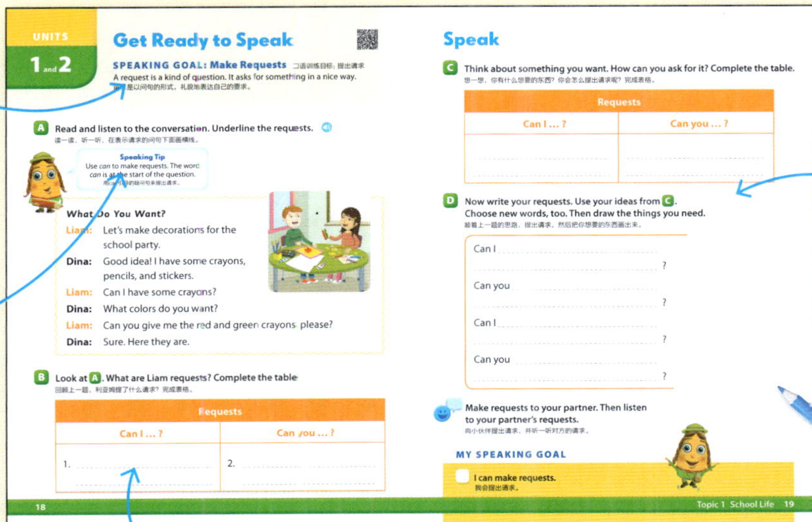

提供"脚手架式"口语交际模板，帮助学生达成口语训练目标。

以思维导图的形式展示口语交际模板，帮助学生梳理思路。

练习册

设置形式多样的练习，帮助学生进一步运用所学的听力学习策略，提高听力理解能力。

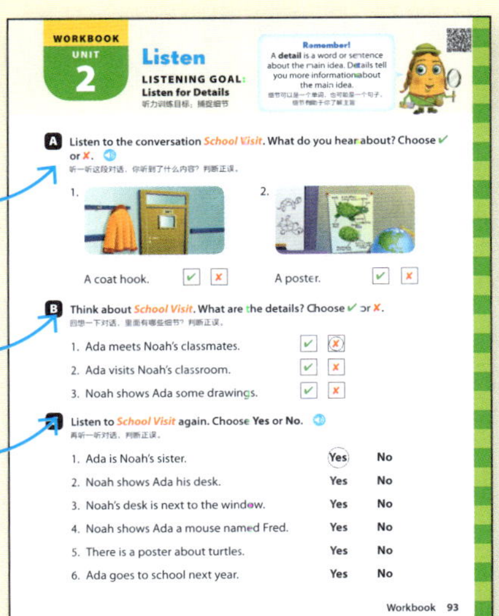

设置丰富的词汇练习，帮助学生提高听力理解和词汇运用能力。

引导学生在交流中使用规范、通顺的语言。

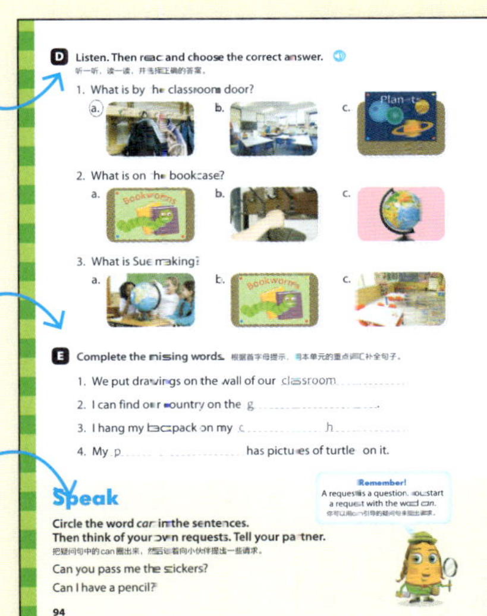

TOPIC

1 School Life

SOCIAL STUDIES

MY GOALS

UNIT 1

- Listen to the conversation *A Busy First Day*
- Listen for the main idea

UNIT 2

- Listen to the story *Guess What?*
- Listen for details

SPEAK

- Make requests

A **Look at the picture. What do you see?**
看图片，回答问题。

1. Where are the children? What are they doing?
2. Is your classroom like this? Why or why not?

FUN FACT

Listen

Classrooms Around the World

B **Listen to the Fun Fact. Then answer the questions.** 听“奇闻趣事”，回答问题。

1. Where is the school?
2. What do you like about the school? Why?

Think, Pair, Share
What is your favorite thing about your school? Why?
你最喜欢你们学校的哪一点？为什么？

UNIT 1

Get Ready to Listen

A Listen, point, and say. Write the words in your picture dictionary.

听一听，指一指，说一说。在“图解词典”中写出对应的单词。

classmates

decorations

drawing

sticker

B Listen and color. 听一听，涂一涂。

C Listen and write. 听一听，写一写。

1. decorations
2. ______
3. ______
4. ______

Listen

LISTENING GOAL: Listen for the Main Idea 听力训练目标：明确主旨

The main idea gives more information about the topic. Listen for the main idea in the first sentence. 主旨提供了更多与话题有关的信息。注意听第一句话，通常第一句话就是主旨句。

A **Listen. Then complete the sentences.**
听一听，并补全句子。

1. This is a picture of the boy's ___cat___.
2. The girl is talking about her ______.
3. The boy is at ______.

A Busy First Day

B **Listen to the conversation *A Busy First Day*. What is it about? Choose the correct picture.** 听一听这段对话讲了什么内容，并选择相应的图片。

A

☐

B

☐

Now put the sentences in order. 给句子排序。

a. Zoe draws a guitar. ☐
b. Jon puts stickers on his dinosaur. ☐
c. Ann puts paper flowers on the tree. 1

What is the **main idea**?
这段对话的主旨是什么？

Think! Do you make decorations at school? What do you like to make?
你在学校做过装饰吗？你喜欢做什么装饰呢？

Understand

A Think about ***A Busy First Day***. What is the main idea?

回想一下对话，对话的主旨是什么?

☐ a. The students are making a learning tree on the first day of school.

☐ b. The students are drawing pictures of a tree on the first day of school.

Remember!
Listen for the **main idea** in the first sentence.
通常第一句话就是主旨句。

B Listen to ***A Busy First Day*** again. Choose the correct answer.

再听一听对话，圈出正确的答案。

1. Zoe and Jon are **at home** / **at school**.
2. Ann's decorations are **flowers** / **flags**.
3. The decorations are **orange** / **pink**.
4. Jon makes a **dinosaur** / **flower**.
5. Zoe makes **a drawing** / **some stickers**.

C Listen. Complete each sentence with a key word. Then match.

听一听，用本单元的重点词汇补全句子，并与相应的图片配对。

1. They are my favorite ___classmates___.
2. Those are our ____________.
3. We have a lot of ____________.
4. You can see my ____________ on my desk.

a. ____ 

b. __1__ 

c. ____ 

d. ____ 

D Listen to ***A Busy First Day*** again. Work with a partner. Complete the diagram. 再听一听对话，和小伙伴一起完成思维导图。

decorations	~~drawing~~	pencil	stickers

that

1. drawing
2. ______

those

3. ______
4. ______

E Look at **D**. Write. Use *that* or *those*. 回顾上一题，用that或those完成句子。

1. 

Is ___that___ your drawing?

2. 

______ are my friend's stickers.

3. 

______ is my green pencil.

4. 

What are ______?

MY LISTENING GOALS

☐ I can listen to the conversation. 我能听懂这段对话。

☐ I can listen for the main idea. 我能明确对话的主旨。

UNIT **2**

Get Ready to Listen

Let's learn the **key words**.
一起来学习重点词汇吧！

A Listen, point, and say. Write the words in your picture dictionary.

听一听，指一指，说一说。在“图解词典”中写出对应的单词或短语。

classroom

coat hooks

globe

poster

B Listen and number. 听一听，在圆圈里填上正确的序号。

C Listen and complete the sentences. 听一听，并补全句子。

1. They are making a __poster__ for the wall.
2. My teacher has a __________ on her desk.
3. Our __________ is very big.
4. My __________ is next to the door.

Listen

LISTENING GOAL: Listen for Details 听力训练目标：捕捉细节

A detail is a word or a sentence about the main idea. Listen for details to learn more information about the main idea. 细节可以是一个单词，也可能是一个句子。注意听细节，这有助于我们了解主旨。

A Listen. Choose ✔ or ✘. 听一听，并判断正误。

1.

✔ ✘

2.

✔ ✘

3.

✔ ✘

Guess What?

B Listen to the story *Guess What?*. Choose the correct picture.
听一听这个故事讲了什么内容，并选择相应的图片。

A

B

Now choose ✔ or ✘. 判断正误。

1. Two people talk in the story. ✔ ✘
2. They talk about school. ✔ ✘
3. The students are playing a game. ✔ ✘

What are the **details**?
故事中有哪些细节？

Think! Do you play games at school? Tell your partner.
你在学校做游戏吗？和小伙伴讲一讲吧。

Understand

Remember!
Listen for **details**. Details tell you more about the main idea.
注意听细节，细节有助于你了解主旨。

A Think about *Guess What?*. Are these details? Choose Yes or No.

回想一下故事，下列句子是细节吗？判断正误。

1. There is a poster in the classroom. **Yes** **No**
2. The children are playing a game. **Yes** **No**

B Listen to *Guess What?* again. Choose the correct answer.

再听一听故事，选择正确的答案。

1. When do the children play the game?
   ☐ a. At the beginning of class. ☑ b. At the end of class.
2. The teacher says *big and round*. The students think it is ________.
   ☐ a. a ball ☐ b. a globe
3. What is on the wall?
   ☐ a. A poster. ☐ b. A drawing.

C Listen and choose the correct picture. Then write the key words.

听一听，选择恰当的图片，并将相应的词写在下方的横线上。

1.  ☑ a  ☐ b

classroom

2. 

☐ a 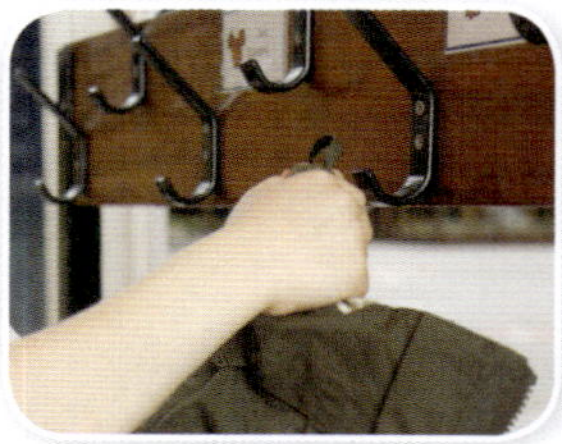 ☐ b

____

3.  ☐ a  ☐ b

____

4.  ☐ a 

☐ b

____

D Listen to *Guess What?* again. Work with a partner. Complete the diagram.

再听一听故事，和小伙伴一起完成思维导图。

Is it / Are they … ?		Yes, it is. / Yes, they are.
1. Is it a globe?	→	Yes, it is.
2. ________ coat hooks?	→	________
3. ________ a poster?	→	________
4. ________ a classroom?	→	________

E Look at D. Write. Use *Is it* or *Are they* for the questions.

回顾上一题，用Is it或Are they完成问句并写出回答。

1. 

Is it a globe?

Yes, it is.

2. 

________ coat hooks?

____

3. 

________ a poster?

____

4. 

________ a classroom?

____

MY LISTENING GOALS

- ☐ **I can listen to the story.** 我能听懂这个故事。
- ☐ **I can listen for details.** 我会捕捉细节。

UNITS
1 and 2

Listening Check

Remember!
Listen for the **main idea**. What is the main idea?
Listen for the **details**. What do they tell you?
注意听主旨，听力材料的主旨是什么？注意听细节，它们告诉了你什么？

A Listen to the conversation *Happy New Year*. What is it about? Choose the correct picture. 听一听这段对话讲了什么内容，并选择相应的图片。

A

☐

B

☐

C

☐

B Do the sentences have the main idea? Choose ✔ or ✘.

下列句子是主旨吗？判断正误。

1. Amy has a party for Lunar New Year. ✔ (✘)
2. Amy and her classmate are making decorations. ✔ ✘
3. Lee tells Amy how to make a lamp. ✔ ✘
4. Amy makes a New Year cake. ✔ ✘

C Do the sentences have the details? Choose ✔ or ✘.

下列句子是细节吗？判断正误。

1. Amy is at home. ✔ (✘)
2. Lee makes a paper lamp. ✔ ✘
3. Amy's poster is on the wall. ✔ ✘
4. Lee's drawing is about a cake. ✔ ✘

D Listen to *Happy New Year* again. Choose the correct answer.

再听一听对话，选择正确的答案。

1. Why are Amy and Lee making decorations?
   - ☐ a. For her birthday. ☑ b. For a special day. ☐ c. For art class.
2. What decorations does Lee make?
   - ☐ a. Paper lamps. ☐ b. A pen. ☐ c. A picture.
3. What animal is on the poster?
   - ☐ a. A dog. ☐ b. A cat. ☐ c. A rabbit.
4. What does Lee do first to make the decoration?
   - ☐ a. Cut lines. ☐ b. Get paper. ☐ c. Open paper.
5. What is Lee's drawing about?
   - ☐ a. A cake. ☐ b. Some fruit. ☐ c. An animal.

E Listen to *Happy New Year* again. Complete the sentences.

再听一听对话，并补全句子。

Amy and Lee are (1) classmates. They make (2) ________ for Lunar New Year. Lunar means *moon*.

Amy: What are those decorations, Lee?

Lee: They're paper lamps.

Amy: How do you make them?

Lee: First, get some paper. Then, cut some lines. Next, open the paper. Last, glue the paper together.

Amy: Wow! I like it! Is that your rabbit (3) ________, Lee?

Lee: Yes, it is. It's the Year of the Rabbit!

Amy: Nice! What's the (4) ________?

Lee: It's a cake. I love New Year's cake! Yum!

UNITS 1 and 2

Get Ready to Speak

SPEAKING GOAL: Make Requests 口语训练目标：提出请求

A request is a kind of question. It asks for something in a nice way.
请求是以问句的形式，礼貌地表达自己的要求。

A Read and listen to the conversation. Underline the requests.
读一读，听一听，在表示请求的问句下面画横线。

Speaking Tip
Use *can* to make requests. The word *can* is at the start of the question.
用can引导的疑问句来提出请求。

What Do You Want?

Liam: Let's make decorations for the school party.

Dina: Good idea! I have some crayons, pencils, and stickers.

Liam: Can I have some crayons?

Dina: What colors do you want?

Liam: Can you give me the red and green crayons, please?

Dina: Sure. Here they are.

B Look at **A**. What are Liam requests? Complete the table.
回顾上一题，利亚姆提了什么请求？完成表格。

Requests	
Can I ... ?	Can you ... ?
1. ______ ______	2. ______ ______

Speak

C **Think about something you want. How can you ask for it? Complete the table.**

想一想，你有什么想要的东西？你会怎么提出请求呢？完成表格。

Requests	
Can I … ?	Can you … ?

D **Now write your requests. Use your ideas from C. Choose new words, too. Then draw the things you need.**

顺着上一题的思路，提出请求，然后把你想要的东西画出来。

Can I ________________________________

____?

Can you ______________________________

____?

Can I ________________________________

____?

Can you ______________________________

____?

Make requests to your partner. Then listen to your partner's requests.

向小伙伴提出请求，并听一听对方的请求。

MY SPEAKING GOAL

☐ **I can make requests.**

我会提出请求。

TOPIC

2

HEALTH

Games Are Fun!

MY GOALS

UNIT 3

- Listen to the story *A Time for Sports*
- Listen for action words

UNIT 4

- Listen to the passage *A Fun Hobby*
- Listen for gist

SPEAK

- Describe routines

A Look at the picture. What do you see?

看图片，回答问题。

1. Where are the children?
2. Where do you play games like this? When?

FUN FACT

Listen

Zorbing

B **Listen to the Fun Fact. Then answer the questions.** 听“奇闻趣事”，回答问题。

1. How does zorbing work?
2. Do you want to try zorbing? Why or why not?

Think, Pair, Share
What games do you play?
你喜欢玩什么游戏？

UNIT 3

Get Ready to Listen

A Listen, point, and say. Write the words in your picture dictionary.

听一听，指一指，说一说。在“图解词典”中写出对应的单词。

jump

run

swing

walk

B Listen and color. 听一听，涂一涂。

C Listen and write. 听一听，写一写。

1. swing
2. ____________
3. ____________
4. ____________

Listen

LISTENING GOAL: Listen for Action Words 听力训练目标：听清行为动词

Words like *run*, *jump*, and *swing* are action words. Listen for action words to know what the people in a story are doing. 行为动词就是表示动作的词，例如run、jump和swing就是行为动词。注意听行为动词，了解故事中的人正在做什么。

A **Listen. Then complete the sentences.** 听一听，并补全句子。

1. Kim plays soccer and ___runs___ with the ball.
2. Pedro ________ to school with his friends.
3. Sue ________ into the water with her sister.

A Time for Sports

B **Listen to the story *A Time for Sports*. What is it about? Choose the correct picture.** 听一听这个故事讲了什么内容，并选择相应的图片。

A

B

Now put the sentences in order. 给句子排序。

a. Adam and Beth see some men running. ☐

b. Adam shows Beth the games. 1

c. They see a man jumping. ☐

What is the most important idea?
这个故事最想表达什么？

Think! Do you like watching games or playing games? Why?
你喜欢看比赛还是参加比赛？为什么？

Understand

A Think about ***A Time for Sports***. What actions do the people do?
回想一下故事，里面的人都做了哪些动作？

☐ a. They run, jump, and swing.
☐ b. They walk, swim, and skip.

Remember!
Action words show what people are doing.
行为动词告诉我们故事中的人正在做什么。

B Listen to ***A Time for Sports*** again. Choose the correct answer.
再听一听故事，圈出正确的答案。

1. Beth and Adam are watching people play **games** / **soccer**.
2. Beth and Adam see **a woman** / **some men** first.
3. Those men can **walk** / **run** really fast.
4. Next, Beth and Adam see a man **run** / **jump.**
5. Beth **can** / **can't** swing.

C Listen. Complete each sentence with a key word. Then match.
听一听，用本单元的重点词汇补全句子，并与相应的图片配对。

1. They __walk__ to school.
2. She ________ in the park.
3. Don't ________ in class!
4. Ceci can ________ high.

a. ____

b. ____

c. ____

d. __1__

D Listen to *A Time for Sports* again. What can the people do? Work with a partner. Complete the diagram.

再听一听故事，里面的人都能做些什么？和小伙伴一起完成思维导图。

Can he / she / they ... ?

1. Can she see?
2. ________ run?
3. ________ jump?
4. ________ swing?

E Look at D. Write. Use *Can he, Can she,* or *Can they*.

回顾上一题，用Can he、Can she或Can they写问句。

1. 

Can she see?

Yes, she can.

2. 

____

Yes, they can.

3. 

____

Yes, he can.

4. 

____

No, she can't.

MY LISTENING GOALS

- [ ] I can listen to the story. 我能听懂这个故事。
- [ ] I can listen for action words to know what people in the story are doing. 我能听清行为动词，从而了解故事中的人正在做什么。

UNIT

4

Get Ready to Listen

Let's learn the **key** **words**.
一起来学习重点词汇吧！

A Listen, point, and say. Write the words in your picture dictionary.

听一听，指一指，说一说。在“图解词典”中写出对应的单词。

hobby

hop

rollerblade

sports

B Listen and number. 听一听，在圆圈里填上正确的序号。

C Listen and complete the sentences. 听一听，并补全句子。

1. My brother and I can ___hop___ fast.
2. We __________ at the park on Saturday.
3. I have a fun __________.
4. We play many __________ at school.

Listen

LISTENING GOAL: Listen for Gist 听力训练目标：把握大意

The gist is what a listening passage is mostly about. To know the gist, listen for names, action words, and places. Also, look at the pictures, title, and activity questions. 大意就是听力材料的主要内容。要把握大意，就要认真听录音中的人名、行为动词和地点。此外，图片、标题和问题也能给我们一些提示。

A Listen. Choose ✔ or ✘. 听一听，并判断正误。

1.

✔ ✘

2.

✔ ✘

3.

✔ ✘

A Fun Hobby

B Listen to the passage *A Fun Hobby*. What is it about? Choose the correct picture.
听一听这篇文章讲了什么内容，并选择相应的图片。

A

☐

B

☐

Now choose ✔ or ✘. 判断正误。

1. Jade rollerblades in many ways. ✔ ✘
2. Jade is learning to rollerblade. ✔ ✘
3. The passage is about school. ✔ ✘

How can you know the **gist** of the passage?
怎样快速把握文章的大意？

Think! Do you have a fun hobby? What is it? What do you like about it?
你有什么有趣的爱好吗？是什么呢？你为什么喜欢它？

Understand

A Think about *A Fun Hobby*. What is the gist? Choose Yes or No.

回想一下文章，它的大意是什么？判断正误。

1. Jade only likes to rollerblade at the park with her friends. **Yes** **No**
2. Jade rollerblades in many ways and in many places. **Yes** **No**

Remember!
Listen for **gist** to find out what a passage is mostly about.
注意听大意，了解文章是关于什么的。

B Listen to *A Fun Hobby* again. Choose the correct answer.

再听一听文章，选择正确的答案。

1. How does Jade rollerblade?
   ☐ a. She can run. ☑ b. She can jump.
2. Why does Jade rollerblade to school?
   ☐ a. It's fast. ☐ b. She can race.
3. Why does Jade like to rollerblade?
   ☐ a. She likes to make new friends. ☐ b. It's fun and good for her.

C Listen and choose the correct picture. Then write the key word.

听一听，选择恰当的图片，并将相应的词写在下方的横线上。

1.

☑ a

☐ b

rollerblade

2.

☐ a

☐ b

____

3.

☐ a

☐ b

____

4.

☐ a

☐ b

____

D Listen to *A Fun Hobby* again. What does Jade like? What doesn't she like? Work with a partner. Complete the diagram.

再听一听文章，雅德喜欢什么、不喜欢什么？和小伙伴一起完成思维导图。

Jade

likes
1. to rollerblade
2. ____________

doesn't like
3. ____________
4. ____________

E Look at D. Write. Use *Yes, she does* or *No, she doesn't*.

回顾上一题，用Yes, she does或No, she doesn't回答问题。

1. 

Does Jade like to rollerblade?

Yes, she does.

2. 

Does Jade like to walk?

____

3. 

Does Jade like to go fast?

____

4. 

Does Jade like to go slow?

____

MY LISTENING GOALS

- [ ] I can listen to the passage. 我能听懂这篇文章。
- [ ] I can listen for the gist of the passage. 我能把握文章的大意。

UNITS **3** and **4**

Listening Check

Remember!
Listen for **action words**. What are the main action words?
Listen for **gist**. What words tell you the gist of a passage?
注意听材料中有哪些行为动词？哪些词能帮助你把握大意？

A Listen to the conversation *A New Sport*. What is it about? Choose the correct picture. 听一听这段对话讲了什么内容，并选择相应的图片。

A

B

C

B Which sentences have action words? Choose ✔ or ✘.
下列句子中有行为动词吗？判断正误。

1. I run fast. ✔ ✘
2. I don't like basketball. ✔ ✘
3. I jump high. ✔ ✘
4. It's fun! ✔ ✘

C What is the gist of the conversation? Choose ✔ or ✘.
这段对话的大意是什么？判断正误。

1. Luke plays soccer and tennis. ✔ ✘
2. Luke wants to try a new sport. ✔ ✘
3. Tony and Luke make a new friend. ✔ ✘
4. Luke and Tony are friends. ✔ ✘

D Listen to *A New Sport* again. Choose the correct answer.

再听一听对话，选择正确的答案。

1. What day does Luke play tennis?

☐ a. On Monday. ☐ b. On Tuesday. ☑ c. On Friday.

2. Who does Luke talk to?

☐ a. His brother. ☐ b. His friend. ☐ c. A teacher.

3. What can Luke do?

☐ a. Hop. ☐ b. Rollerblade. ☐ c. Jump high.

4. Which sport doesn't Luke like?

☐ a. Basketball. ☐ b. Soccer. ☐ c. Tennis.

5. What can Jade do?

☐ a. Jump. ☐ b. Rollerblade. ☐ c. Dance.

E Listen to *A New Sport* again. Complete the sentences.

再听一听对话，并补全句子。

Luke plays (1) ___sports___ at school. He plays soccer on Tuesday and tennis on Friday. Now he wants to try a new sport. He talks to his friend, Tony.

Luke: Let's try a new sport, Tony.

Tony: OK! What can you do?

Luke: I (2) __________ fast. I (3) __________ high.

Tony: Hmm. Do you like basketball?

Luke: No, I don't.

Tony: Hey, Jade! We want to try a new sport. What can you do?

Jade: Well, I can (4) __________ fast!

Tony: Let's try to rollerblade!

Luke: OK! Let's do it!

UNITS 3 and 4

Get Ready to Speak

SPEAKING GOAL: Describe Routines

口语训练目标：描述生活常规

Routines are the things you do often. Routines describe what you do and when. 生活常规就是你经常做的事，生活常规体现了你会在什么时间做什么。

A Read and listen to the routine. Underline the time phrases.

读一读，听一听，在表示时间的短语下面画横线。

Speaking Tip

Use time phrases like *every Monday*, *Wednesday to Friday*, and *on the weekend* to show when.

用表示时间的短语，比如 every Monday、Wednesday to Friday 或者 on the weekend表明时间。

My Weekly Routine

by Jane

I do karate every Monday. From Wednesday to Friday, I run in the mornings. But I don't play sports on the weekend. I walk in the park with my friends. And I ride my bike. I sleep a lot, too.

B Look at **A**. What is Jane's routine? Complete the diagram.

回顾上一题，简的生活常规是怎样的？完成思维导图。

My Weekly Routine

1. Monday	2. Wednesday to Friday	3. Weekend
do karate	______	______

Speak

C Think about sports you play or hobbies you do. What is your routine? Complete the diagram.

想一想你的爱好以及你经常做的运动。你的生活常规是怎样的？完成思维导图。

My Weekly Routine

________	________ to ________	Weekend
________	________	________

D Now write your routine. Use your ideas from **C**. Choose new words, too. Then draw yourself playing your sport or doing your hobby.

顺着上一题的思路，把你的生活常规写下来，然后把你的爱好或者你做的运动画出来。

On ________, ________________
________________________________.

From ________ to ________,
________________________________.

On the weekend, ________________
________________________________.

Ask your partner about his or her routine. Then tell your partner your routine to your partner.

和小伙伴聊一聊他 / 她的生活常规，并和对方分享你的生活常规。

MY SPEAKING GOAL

☐ **I can describe a routine.**

我会描述生活常规。

TOPIC
3 It's Shopping Time!

MATH

MY GOALS

UNIT 5

- Listen to the story *A Gift for Mom*
- Listen for prices

UNIT 6

- Listen to the announcement *Megamarket*
- Listen for days of the week

SPEAK

- Exchange information

A **Look at the picture. What do you see?**
看图片，回答问题。

1. Where is the woman? What is she doing?
2. Where does your family go shopping?

B **Listen to the Fun Fact. Then answer the questions.** 听“奇闻趣事”，回答问题。

1. What kind of place is it?
2. Do you want to go there? Why or why not?

Think, Pair, Share
What things do you like to buy?
你喜欢买什么东西?

UNIT **5**

Get Ready to Listen

A Listen, point, and say. Write the words in your picture dictionary.

听一听，指一指，说一说。在“图解词典”中写出对应的单词。

clothes

smartphone

T-shirt

vase

B Listen and color. 听一听，涂一涂。

C Listen and write. 听一听，写一写。

1. clothes
2. ______
3. ______
4. ______

Listen

LISTENING GOAL: Listen for Prices 听力训练目标：明确价格

Words like *dollars* and *cents* tell you about prices. Listen for numbers and price words to find out how much something is.

像dollars和cents这样的单词能给你价格提示。注意听录音中的数字和货币单位，了解商品的价格。

A **Listen. Choose the correct answer.** 听一听，在听到的价格前打钩。

1. ☑ a. 20 dollars ☐ b. 30 dollars
2. ☐ a. 12 dollars ☐ b. 10 dollars
3. ☐ a. 90 cents ☐ b. 19 cents

A Gift for Mom

B **Listen to the story *A Gift for Mom*. What is it about? Choose the correct picture.**

听一听这个故事讲了什么内容，并选择相应的图片。

A

☐

B

☐

Now put the sentences in order. 给句子排序。

a. Tara shows the sales clerk a picture of her mom. ☐

b. Tara can buy the small vase. ☐

c. Tara talks to the sales clerk. 1

What **prices** do you hear?
你听到了哪些价格？

Think!

How do you pay for things in a store? What do you do when you don't have enough money?

你在商店买东西时怎么付款？如果带的现金不够，你会怎么做？

Understand

Remember!
Price words, like *dollars* and *cents*, tell you how much something is.
像dollars和cents这样的货币单位能给你价格提示。

A Think about ***A Gift for Mom***. What do the price words tell you?
回想一下故事，里面提到了什么商品的价格?

☐ a. They tell you how much the vases are.
☐ b. They tell you how much the T-shirts are.

B Listen to ***A Gift for Mom*** again. Choose the correct answer.
再听一听故事，圈出正确的答案。

1. Tara is at a **mall** / **market**.
2. Tara is with her **mom** / **father**.
3. Tara's mom has red **hair** / **clothes**.
4. Tara has 10 **cents** / **dollars**.
5. Tara buys a **small** / **large** vase.

C Listen. Complete each sentence with a key word. Then match.
听一听，用本单元的重点词汇补全句子，并与相应的图片配对。

1. My mom likes clothes.
2. This is my new ________.
3. My mom doesn't like ________.
4. There are ________ in the market.

a. ____ 

b. ____ 

c. 1 

d. ____ 

D Listen to *A Gift for Mom* again. Complete the diagram.

再听一听故事，完成思维导图。

Does she have / like ... ?	Yes	No
1. clothes	✔	
2. red hair		
3. nice shirt		
4. vase		

E Look at D. Write. Use *Yes, she does* or *No, she doesn't*.

回顾上一题，用Yes, she does或No, she doesn't回答问题。

1. 

Does she like clothes?

Yes, she does.

2. 

Does she have red hair?

____

3. 

Does she have a nice shirt?

____

4. 

Does she have a vase?

____

MY LISTENING GOALS

- ☐ **I can listen to the story.** 我能听懂这个故事。
- ☐ **I can listen for prices to find out how much something is.** 我能明确商品的价格。

UNIT

6 Get Ready to Listen

Let's learn the **key words.**
一起来学习重点词汇吧！

A Listen, point, and say. Write the words in your picture dictionary.

听一听，指一指，说一说。在“图解词典”中写出对应的单词。

camera

plane

shopping cart

toy

B Listen and number. 听一听，在圆圈里填上正确的序号。

C Listen and complete the sentences. 听一听，并补全句子。

1. There are a lot of ____toys____ in the store.
2. That ____________ is dirty.
3. My brother's ____________ is black.
4. Tom has a small ____________.

Listen

LISTENING GOAL: Listen for Days of the Week 听力训练目标：听清是星期几

Words like *Monday* and *Wednesday* are days of the week. Listen for days to know when something happens. 像Monday和Wednesday这样的单词是英文中表示星期几的词。注意听这些词，确定事情发生的时间。

A **Listen and complete the sentences.** 听一听，并补全句子。

1. The toy store isn't open on ___Sunday___.
2. The boy's birthday is on ________.
3. The girl has an art class on ________.

Megamarket

B **Listen to the announcement *Megamarket*. What is it about? Choose the correct picture.**
听一听这则公告讲了什么内容，并选择相应的图片。

A

B

Now choose ✔ or ✘. 判断正误。

1. The man says it's Monday. ✔ ✘
2. Cameras are four dollars. ✔ ✘
3. The man talks about clothes. ✔ ✘

What **days** does the man mention in the announcement?
公告中提到了哪几天？

Think!
Do you hear announcements at stores?
What do the announcements say?
你在商店里听到过公告吗？那些公告都讲了什么内容？

Understand

A Think about *Megamarket*. What days do you hear? Choose Yes or No. 回想一下公告，你听到了哪些日期？判断正误。

1. Monday. **Yes** **No**
2. Thursday. **Yes** **No**

Remember!
Days tell you when something happens.
表示星期几的词能告诉你事情发生的时间。

B Listen to *Megamarket* again. Choose the correct answer.
再听一听公告，选择正确的答案。

1. What day can you buy planes for five dollars?
   ☑ a. On Tuesday. ☐ b. On Friday.
2. What day can you buy ice cream at a good price?
   ☐ a. On Sunday. ☐ b. On Saturday.
3. How much is the ice cream?
   ☐ a. 25 cents. ☐ b. 99 cents.

C Listen and choose the correct picture. Then write the key word.
听一听，选择恰当的图片，并将相应的词写在下方的横线上。

1\.

☑ a

☐ b

plane

2\.

☐ a

☐ b

____

3\.

☐ a

☐ b

____

4\.

☐ a

☐ b

____

D Listen to *Megamarket* again. Work with a partner. Complete the table.

再听一听公告，和小伙伴一起完成表格。

1. cameras →	camera store
2. planes →	________
3. paint →	________
4. ice cream →	________

E Look at D. Write. Use *It's* or *They're*. 回顾上一题，用It's或They're完成句子。

1. 

Where are the cameras?

They're in the camera store.

2. 

Where are the planes?

________ in the toy store.

3. 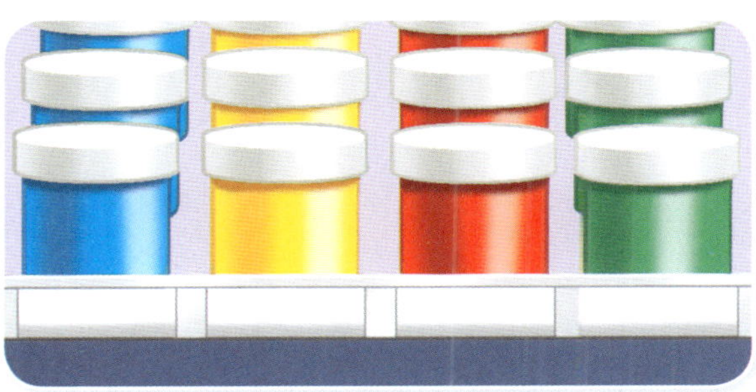

Where is the paint?

________ in the art store.

4. 

Where is the ice cream?

________ in the ice cream store.

MY LISTENING GOALS

- [ ] I can listen to the announcement. 我能听懂这则公告。
- [ ] I can listen for days of the week. 我能听清是星期几。

UNITS
5 and 6

Listening Check

Remember!
Listen for numbers and **price words**. What are the prices?
Listen for **days of the week**. What do they tell you?
注意听数字和货币单位，商品的价格分别是多少？注意听表示星期几的词，它们告诉了你什么？

A Listen to the passage *The Grand Bazaar*. What is it about? Choose the correct picture.

听一听这篇文章讲了什么内容，并选择相应的图片。

A
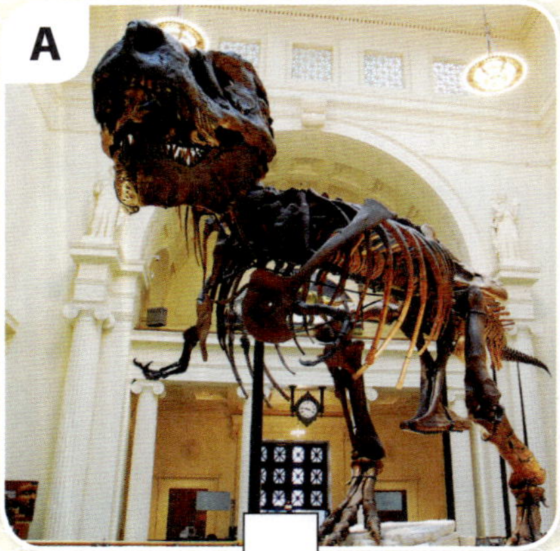
☐

B

☐

C

☐

B Are the prices correct? Choose ✔ or ✘.

下列句子中的价格正确吗？根据听到的内容判断正误。

1. The T-shirt is 5 dollars. ✔ ✘
2. The T-shirt is 50 dollars. ✔ ✘
3. The candy is 50 cents. ✔ ✘
4. The candy is 15 cents. ✔ ✘

C Are the days correct? Choose ✔ or ✘.

下列句子中的日期正确吗？根据听到的内容判断正误。

1. They go to the market on Saturday. ✔ ✘
2. They go to the market on Tuesday. ✔ ✘
3. Their friend's birthday is on Sunday. ✔ ✘
4. Their friend's birthday is on Monday. ✔ ✘

D Listen to *The Grand Bazaar* again. Choose the correct answer.

再听一听文章，选择正确的答案。

1. What is the Grand Bazaar?

   ☐ a. A mall. ☑ b. A market. ☐ c. A store.

2. Who does Ian go to the Grand Bazaar with?

   ☐ a. His brother. ☐ b. His dad. ☐ c. His friend.

3. What do they want to buy at the market?

   ☐ a. A gift. ☐ b. Toys. ☐ c. Paint.

4. What does Ata buy?

   ☐ a. A smartphone. ☐ b. Some candy. ☐ c. A T-shirt.

5. What does Ian buy?

   ☐ a. A T-shirt. ☐ b. Some candy. ☐ c. A plane.

E Listen to *The Grand Bazaar* again. Complete the sentences.

再听一听文章，并补全句子。

The Grand Bazaar is in Turkey. It's an old market with a lot of stores. I go with my friend, Ata. Ata knows all the places! We go on Saturday. It's our friend's birthday on Sunday. We want to buy a birthday gift for our friend here. I like (1) ___toys___. Ata likes (2) ____________. Ata buys a (3) ____________. It's five dollars. I buy some (4) ____________. It's 50 cents! Now, what can we buy for our friend? It's fun to go shopping at the Grand Bazaar!

UNITS 5 and 6

Get Ready to Speak

SPEAKING GOAL: Exchange Information

口语训练目标：交换信息

We tell the things we know. We ask about the things we want to know.

我们说出自己知道的信息、询问自己不了解的信息，进行信息交换。

A **Read and listen to the information. Underline the phrases that ask for more information.** 读一读，听一听，在询问信息的句子下面画横线。

Speaking Tip

Use questions like *What about you?* to learn information about someone.

用问句，比如What about you?来询问关于某人的信息。

What about you?

Tom: What's your favorite store?

Kim: It's the toy store. I can buy scooters there.

Tom: Nice!

Kim: What about you? What's your favorite store?

Tom: I like the clothes store. I can buy T-shirts there.

B **Look at A. What do Tom and Kim say? Complete the table.**

回顾上一题，汤姆和金分别说了什么？完成表格。

	Favorite Store	Things to Buy
Kim		
Tom		

Speak

C **Think about your favorite store. What can you buy there? Complete the table.** 想一想你最喜欢的商店，你能在那里买到什么？完成表格。

Favorite Store	Things to Buy

D **Now write. Share information. Use your ideas from C. Then draw something from the store.**
顺着上一题的思路，进行信息交换，把下面的内容补充完整，然后试着画一画店里的商品。

What's your favorite store?

It's the ________ store.

I can ________________

________________.

What about you?
What's your favorite store?

It's the ________ store.

I can ________________

________________.

Ask your partner about his or her favorite store. Then tell your partner about your favorite store. 问一问小伙伴最喜欢哪家商店，然后和对方分享一下你最喜欢的商店。

MY SPEAKING GOAL

☐ **I can exchange information.**
我会交换信息。

TOPIC

4

GEOGRAPHY

Where Do People Work?

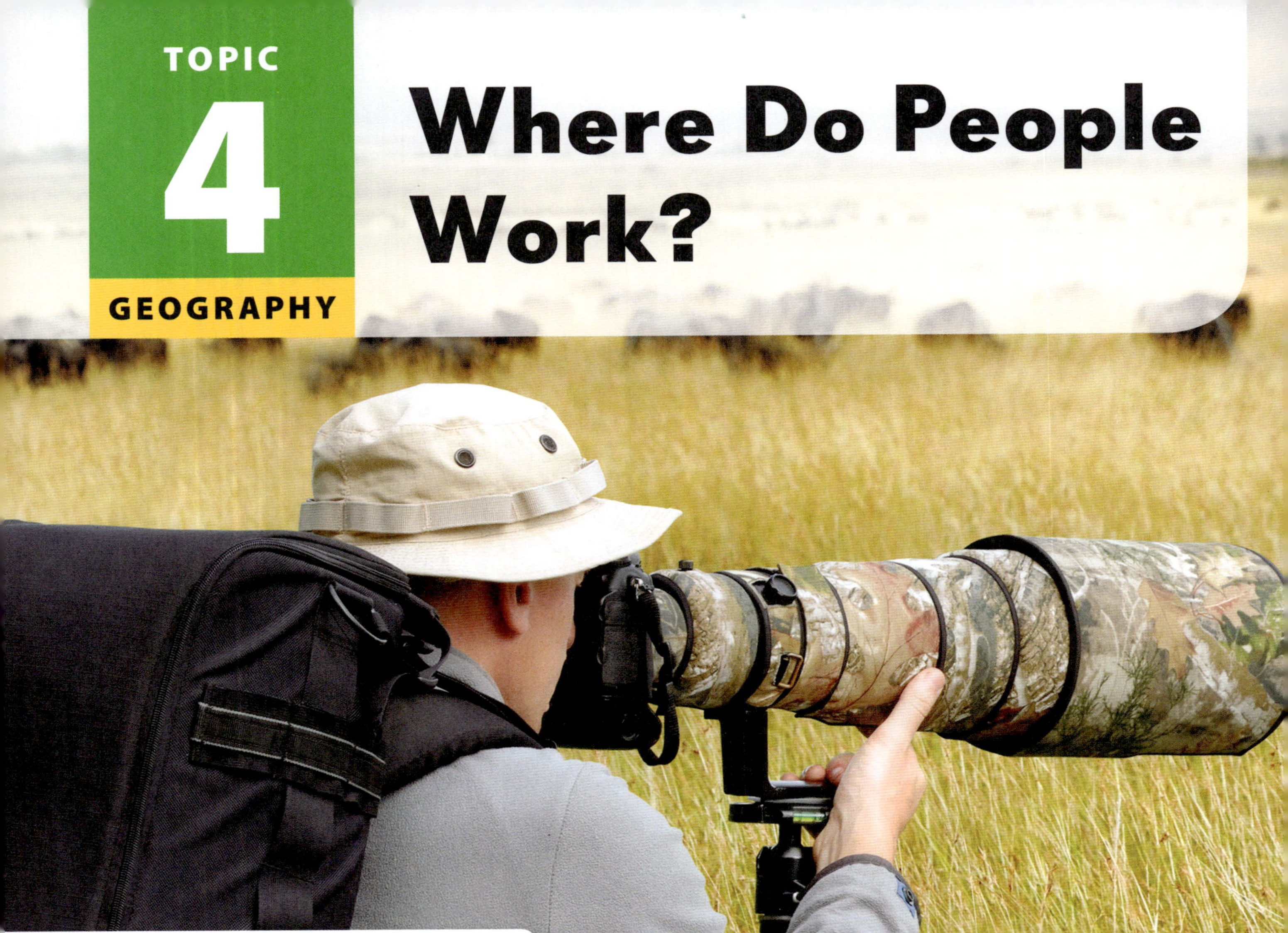

MY GOALS

UNIT 7

- Listen to the interview *Working Around the World*
- Listen for places

UNIT 8

- Listen to the conversation *New Friends*
- Listen for addresses

SPEAK

- Describe a place

A **Look at the picture. What do you see?**
看图片，回答问题。

1. Where is the man? What is he doing?
2. Do people do this in your country? Why or why not?

FUN FACT

Listen

A Wildlife Photographer

B **Listen to the Fun Fact. Then answer the questions.** 听“奇闻趣事”，回答问题。

1. What is the man’s job?
2. Do you like this kind of job? Why or why not?

Think, Pair, Share
What job do you want to do? Why?
你想从事什么工作？为什么？

UNIT

7

Get Ready to Listen

Let's learn the **key words**.
一起来学习重点词汇吧！

A Listen, point, and say. Write the words in your picture dictionary.

听一听，指一指，说一说。在“图解词典”中写出对应的单词。

chef

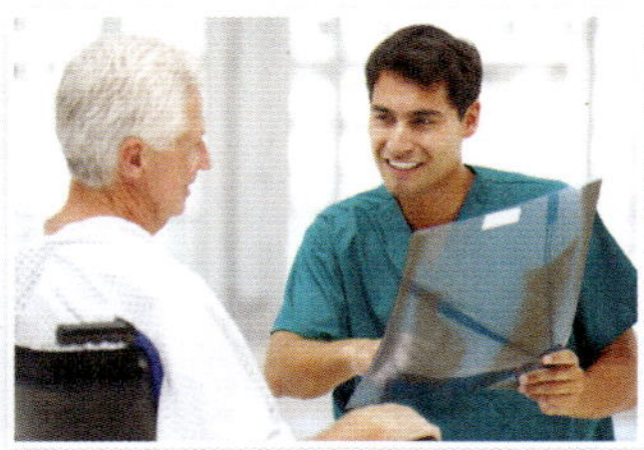

nurse

painter

zookeeper

B Listen and color. 听一听，涂一涂。

C Listen and write. 听一听，写一写。

1. zookeeper
2. ____________
3. ____________
4. ____________

Listen

LISTENING GOAL: Listen for Places 听力训练目标：听清地点

Places are countries, cities, and buildings. *Turkey*, *Seoul*, and *a school* are places.
Listen to places to know where people are. 地点可以是具体的国家、城市或建筑物，例如土耳其、首尔或者学校。注意听这些词，了解人们在哪里。

A **Listen. What is the place? Choose the correct answer.**
听一听。这是什么地方？选择正确的答案。

1. ☐ a. A school. ☑ b. A home.
2. ☐ a. A city. ☐ b. A building.
3. ☐ a. A country. ☐ b. A city.

Working Around the World

B **Listen to the interview *Working Around the World*. What is it about? Choose the correct picture.**
听一听这段采访录音是关于什么的，并选择相应的图片。

A

☐

B

☐

Now put the sentences in order. 给句子排序。

a. Tam talks to a chef. ☐
b. Tam meets Mary and Bill. [1]
c. Tam speaks to a zookeeper. ☐

Where are the people?
What jobs do they do?
这些人在哪里？
他们是做什么工作的？

Think!
What other jobs do you know?
Where do the people work?
你还知道哪些工作？那些人都在哪里工作？

Understand

Remember!
Places can tell you where people are. They can be countries, cities, and buildings.
地点可以是具体的国家、城市或者建筑物。它们能告诉你人们在哪里。

A **Think about *Working Around the World*. What places are in the interview?**
回想一下采访内容，里面提到了哪些地点？

☐ a. Mexico. ☐ b. A restaurant.
☐ c. A school. ☐ d. China.

B **Listen to *Working Around the World* again. Choose the correct answer.**
再听一听录音，圈出正确的答案。

1. Mary helps sick **animals** / **people**.
2. Bill paints **houses** / **pictures**.
3. Raúl works as a **chef** / **teacher**.
4. Meg is a **zookeeper** / **nurse**.
5. Meg works with **people** / **animals**.

C **Listen. Complete each sentence with a key word. Then match.**
听一听，用本单元的重点词汇补全句子，并与相应的图片配对。

1. This is my mom. She's a __painter__.
2. My uncle is a ________. I go see him at work.
3. This is my dad. He's a ________.
4. Aunt Emma is a ________. She's nice.

a. ____

b. ____

c. ____

d. __1__

D Listen to ***Working Around the World*** again. Work with a partner. Complete the table. 再听一听录音，和小伙伴一起完成表格。

Mary	Who is she ?	She's a nurse.
Bill and Tom	Who ______ ?	______ painters.
Raúl	Who ______ ?	______ a chef.
Meg	Who ______ ?	______ a zookeeper.

E Look at **D**. Write. Use *is* or *are*. 回顾上一题，用is或are完成句子。

1. 

Who is she ?

She's a nurse.

2. 

Who ______ ?

______

3. 

Who ______ ?

______

4. 

Who ______ ?

______

MY LISTENING GOALS

- [ ] I can listen to the interview. 我能听懂这段采访录音。
- [ ] I can listen for places to know where people are. 我能听清地点，知道人们在哪里。

UNIT
8
Get Ready to Listen

Let's learn the **key words.**
一起来学习重点词汇吧！

A Listen, point, and say. Write the words in your picture dictionary.
听一听，指一指，说一说。在“图解词典”中写出对应的单词或短语。

barber

librarian

postal worker

server

B Listen and number. 听一听，在圆圈里填上正确的序号。

C Listen and complete the sentences. 听一听，并补全句子。

1. My sister is a __server__.
2. The ________ is in the van.
3. The ________ is at her desk.
4. My dad is a ________ in the city.

Listen

LISTENING GOAL: Listen for Addresses 听力训练目标：听清地址

An address has a number and street name. It shows where a building is. Listen for addresses to know where people live or work.

地址包括街道名称和编号，能表示具体的位置。注意听地址，了解人们在哪里居住或工作。

A **Listen and number.** 听一听，在方框中填上正确的序号。

A

☐

B

☐

C

1

New Friends

B **Listen to the conversation *New Friends*. What is it about? Choose the correct picture.**
听一听这段对话讲了什么内容，并选择相应的图片。

A

☐

B

☐

Now choose ✔ or ✘. 判断正误。

1. The boys talk about people at their school. ✔ ✘
2. Lee tells Han where people work. ✔ ✘
3. Han wants to know where the barber works. ✔ ✘

What do the **addresses** tell you?
地址能告诉你什么信息？

Think!
Do you have these people in your city? Where do they work?
你所在的城市里有做这些工作的人吗？他们在哪里工作？

Understand

Remember!
An **address** has a number and street name. It shows where people live or work.
地址包括街道名称和编号，能告诉你人们在哪里居住或工作。

A Think about *New Friends*. Choose Yes or No.

回想一下对话，判断正误。

1. Brian works at 65 Elm Street. **Yes** **No**
2. Mr. Kim works at 22 Oak Street. **Yes** **No**

B Listen to *New Friends* again. Choose the correct answer.

再听一听对话，选择正确的答案。

1. Who do Han and Lee talk about first?
   - [✔] a. A librarian.
   - [ ] b. A postal worker.
2. Who works at Maple Restaurant?
   - [ ] a. Jack.
   - [ ] b. Brian.
3. What does Mr. Kim do?
   - [ ] a. He's a server.
   - [ ] b. He's a barber.

C Listen and choose the correct picture. Then write the key word.

听一听，选择恰当的图片，并将相应的词写在下方的横线上。

1.

[ ] a

[✔] b

postal worker

2.

[ ] a

[ ] b

______

3.

[ ] a

[ ] b

______

4.

[ ] a

[ ] b

______

D Listen to *New Friends* again. Complete the diagram.

再听一听对话，完成思维导图。

What does he / she do?		Where does he / she work?
1. librarian	→	library
2. ______	→	post office
3. ______	→	restaurant
4. ______	→	barbershop

E Look at D. Write. Use *What* or *Where*. 回顾上一题，用What或Where完成问句。

1. 

Where does she work?

She works in a library.

2. 

______ does he do?

He's a postal worker.

3. 

______ does he work?

He works in a restaurant.

4. 

______ does he do?

He's a barber.

MY LISTENING GOALS

- ☐ I can listen to the conversation. 我能听懂这段对话。
- ☐ I can listen to addresses to know where people live or work. 我能听清地址，从而知道人们在哪里居住或工作。

Listening Check

Remember!
Listen for **places**. Where are the people? Listen for **addresses**. Where do they live or work?
注意听地点，人们在哪里？注意听地址，人们在哪里居住或工作？

A Listen to the conversation *The Guessing Game*. What is it about? Choose the correct picture. 听一听这段对话讲了什么内容，并选择相应的图片。

A ☐

B ☐

C ☐

B Do the sentences have places? Choose ✔ or ✘.

下列句子中有地点吗？判断正误。

1. Ellie and Max are at home. (✔) ✘
2. They work at 24 Park Street. ✔ ✘
3. Max lives at 45 Main Street. ✔ ✘
4. Max's mom works in a restaurant. ✔ ✘

C Do the sentences have addresses? Choose ✔ or ✘.

下列句子中有地址吗？判断正误。

1. Ellie and Max play a game at home. ✔ (✘)
2. The servers work at 24 Park Street. ✔ ✘
3. Max lives at 45 Main Street. ✔ ✘
4. Max's mom is a librarian. ✔ ✘

D Listen to *The Guessing Game* again. Choose the correct answer.

再听一听对话，选择正确的答案。

1. What job does Max guess first?
   - ☐ a. Server. ☑ b. Barber. ☐ c. Postal worker.
2. Who work at 24 Park Street?
   - ☐ a. Barbers. ☐ b. Postal workers. ☐ c. Servers.
3. What is the number of Max's house?
   - ☐ a. 44. ☐ b. 45. ☐ c. 46.
4. Who is a postal worker?
   - ☐ a. Max's dad. ☐ b. Max's mom. ☐ c. Ellie's dad.
5. Where does Max's mom work?
   - ☐ a. At a restaurant. ☐ b. At a library. ☐ c. At a post office.

E Listen to *The Guessing Game* again. Complete the sentences.

再听一听对话，并补全句子。

Ellie and Max play a game at home.

Ellie: Ready? Let's play! They work at 24 Park Street. Who are they?

Max: Hmm. (1) __Barbers__?

Ellie: No. They work in a restaurant.

Max: Are they (2) ________?

Ellie: Yes! Your turn.

Max: OK. This person lives at 45 Main Street.

Ellie: Hmm. I know that address. That's your house!

Max: What does this person do?

Ellie: Is it your mom? She's a (3) ________!

Max: No! My dad's a postal worker! My mom's a (4) ________.

Ellie: You win!

UNITS

7 and 8

Get Ready to Speak

SPEAKING GOAL: Describe a Place 口语训练目标：描述一个地点

You can describe a country, city, or building. Describe where it is and how it looks. 你可以描述一个国家、一座城市或者建筑。说一说它位于哪里，是什么样子的。

A **Read and listen to the description. Underline the location words.**

读一读，听一听，在方位词下面画横线。

Speaking Tip

Words like *in*, *at,* and *on* are location words. Use location words to help you describe where something is.

像in、at、on这样的单词都是方位词。使用方位词有助于你描述事物的具体位置。

The City Hospital

My mom is a nurse. She works at a hospital. The hospital is on Elm Street. It is a big place, and it has a lot of rooms. My mom works on the top floor of the building. She helps sick people.

B **Look at A. How does the girl describe the hospital? Complete the diagram.** 回顾上一题，这个女孩是怎么描述这家医院的？完成思维导图。

The City Hospital

1. It's on Elm Street.
2. ____________
3. ____________

Speak

C **Think about a place that you know. Where is it? What does it look like? Complete the diagram.**

想一个你知道的地方，那个地方是哪里？那里是什么样子的？完成思维导图。

Place

D **Now write a description of your place. Use your ideas from C. Choose new words, too. Then draw the place.**

顺着上一题的思路，描述一下那个地方，然后画一画那个地方。

This is ________________.

It is ________________.

It is a ________________.

It has ________________.

Ask your partner to tell you about his/her place. Then tell your partner about your place.

问一问小伙伴想到的地方是哪里，再把你想到的地方和他讲一讲。

MY SPEAKING GOAL

☐ **I can describe a place.**

我会描述地点。

TOPIC

5 One Day Around the World

SOCIAL STUDIES

MY GOALS

UNIT 9

- Listen to the video call *It's Early!*
- Listen for times

UNIT 10

- Listen to the story *A Great Day*
- Listen for sequence

SPEAK

- Make an appointment

A **Look at the picture. What do you see?**
看图片，回答问题。

1. What can you see on the clock?
2. Do you have a big clock in your city? Where is it?

FUN FACT

Listen

What's the Time?

B **Listen to the Fun Fact. Then answer the questions.** 听“奇闻趣事”，回答问题。

1. What does the World Clock show?
2. How do you check the time in places around the world?

Think, Pair, Share
How do you tell the time?
你怎么确定时间?

UNIT 9

Get Ready to Listen

A Listen, point, and say. Write the words in your picture dictionary.

听一听，指一指，说一说。在“图解词典”中写出对应的单词或短语。

get dressed

morning

walk to school

wash my face

B Listen and color. 听一听，涂一涂。

C Listen and write. 听一听，写一写。

1. walk to school
2. ________
3. ________
4. ________

Listen

LISTENING GOAL: Listen for Times 听力训练目标：明确时间

Examples of times are 7:30 a.m. and 2:00 p.m. Listen for times to know when things happen.
7:30 a.m. 和 2:00 p.m. 都表示时间。注意听表示时间的词，明确事情发生的具体时间。

A **Listen. Then complete the sentences.** 听一听，并补全句子。

1. Kristi has math at 9:00 a.m.
2. Paul gets up at ________
3. Max eats dinner at ________

B **Listen to the video call *It's Early!*. What is it about? Choose the correct picture.**
听一听这通视频电话讲了什么内容，并选择相应的图片。

A

B

Now choose ✔ or ✘. 判断正误。

1. Yen and Li are in the same place. ✔ ✘
2. Li has English class at 3:30 p.m. ✔ ✘
3. Yen washes his face and then gets dressed. ✔ ✘

What do the times tell you?
时间能告诉你什么信息？

Think! When do you talk to your friends on the computer or phone?
你通常什么时候和朋友打电话或者视频通话？

Understand

Remember!
Times tell you when something happens.
表示时间的词能告诉你事情发生的具体时间。

A **Think about *It's Early!*. Read the sentences with times. Choose the correct sentences.**
回想一下视频电话的内容，读下列句子，选择正确的答案。

☐ a. It's 7:00 a.m. in England. It's 3:00 p.m. in Hong Kong.
☐ b. It's 6:30 p.m. in England. It's 2:30 a.m. in Hong Kong.

B **Listen to *It's Early!* again. Choose the correct answer.**
再听一听录音，圈出正确的答案。

1. Yen and Li talk **at school** / **on a video call**.
2. Li is in **Hong Kong** / **England**.
3. In Hong Kong, the time is **7:00 a.m.** / **3:00 p.m.**
4. Li **has English class** / **talks to Yen** at 3:30 p.m.
5. Yen **gets dressed** / **walks to school** at 8:00 a.m.

C **Listen. Complete each sentence with a key word. Then match.**
听一听，用本单元的重点词汇补全句子，并与相应的图片配对。

1. It's __morning__. It's time for breakfast.
2. I ________________ at 6:30 in the morning.
3. She ________________. Then she goes to school.
4. The boys ________________ at 8:00 a.m.

a. ____

b. __1__

c. ____

d. ____

D Listen to *It's Early!* again. Work with a partner. Complete the diagram with the correct times. 再听一听录音，和小伙伴一起填写正确的时间，完成思维导图。

gets up	washes his face	gets dressed	walks to school
1. 6:30 a.m.	2. ______	3. ______	4. ______

E Look at **D**. Write. 回顾上一题，补全句子。

1. 

He ______ gets up ______
at 6:30 a.m.

2. 

He ______________
at 6:45 a.m.

3. 

He ______________
at 7:30 a.m.

4. 

He ______________
at 8:00 a.m.

MY LISTENING GOALS

- ☐ I can listen to the video call. 我能听懂这通视频电话。
- ☐ I can listen for times to know when things happen. 我能明确事情发生的具体时间。

UNIT 10

Get Ready to Listen

A Listen, point, and say. Write the words in your picture dictionary.

听一听，指一指，说一说。在“图解词典”中写出对应的单词。

afternoon

day

evening

sleep

B Listen and number. 听一听，在圆圈里填上正确的序号。

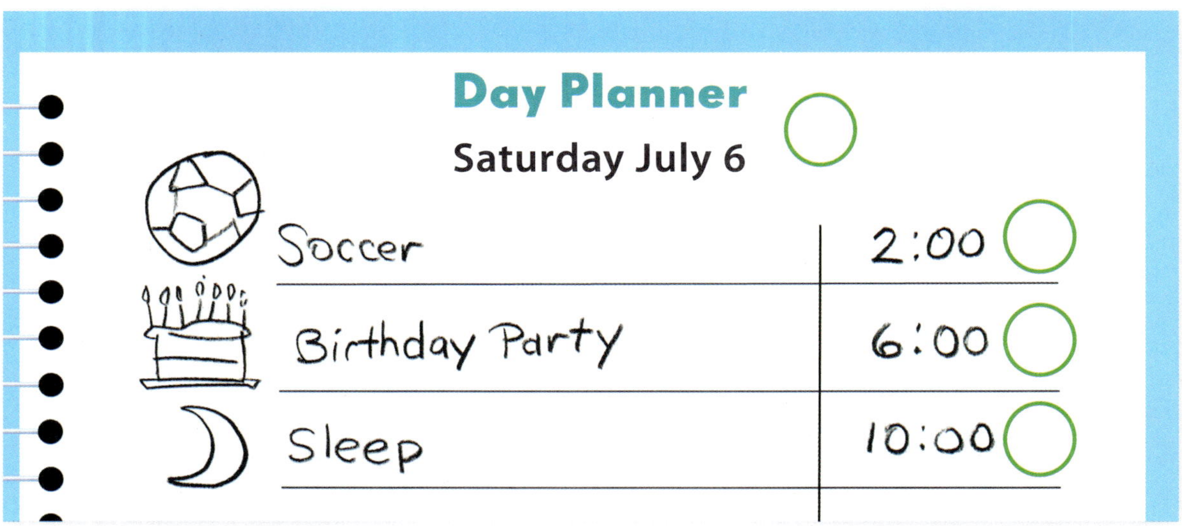

C Listen and complete the sentences. 听一听，并补全句子。

1. Tim walks to school on sunny ___days___.
2. Liz watches TV in the ______.
3. Yoko does homework in the ______.
4. Kim goes to ______ late on Saturday.

Listen

LISTENING GOAL: Listen for Sequence 听力训练目标：理清顺序

The sequence is the order things happen. Listen for words like *first*, *next*, *then*, and *finally* to understand the sequence.

顺序就是事情发生的先后次序。注意听 first、next、then 和 finally 等表示顺序的词，了解事情发生的顺序。

A **Listen. What happens first? Choose the correct answer.**

听一听，哪件事先发生？选择正确的答案。

1. ☑ a. Tim drinks water. ☐ b. Tim eats breakfast.
2. ☐ a. Todd does his homework. ☐ b. Todd goes to the market.
3. ☐ a. Sue talks with her friends. ☐ b. Sue watches TV.

A Great Day

B **Listen to the story *A Great Day*. What is it about? Choose the correct picture.**

听一听这个故事讲了什么内容，并选择相应的图片。

A

☐

B

☐

Now put the sentences in order. 给句子排序。

a. Pam talks to her mom. ☐

b. Pam learns about animals. 1

c. Pam goes home. ☐

Which words show the **sequence** of the day?

哪些词表明了这一天所做之事的顺序？

Think!

Do you take school trips? Where do you go?

你参加过学校的郊游吗？都去了哪里呢？

Understand

Remember!
Listen for **sequence** words. Words like *first*, *next*, *then*, and *finally* help you understand the order of things.
注意听表示顺序的词，例如first、next、then和finally，它们能告诉你事情发生的顺序。

A

Think about *A Great Day*.
Read the sentences. Choose Yes or No.
回想一下故事，读一读句子，判断正误。

1. Pam has a soccer game. Then she eats lunch. **Yes** **No**
2. Pam has a soccer game. Then she walks home. **Yes** **No**

B

Listen to *A Great Day* again. Choose the correct answer.
再听一听故事，选择正确的答案。

1. What does Pam do first on Friday afternoons?
   ☑ a. She eats lunch. ☐ b. She has art class.
2. What does Pam do today?
   ☐ a. She has a soccer game. ☐ b. She goes on a school trip.
3. What does Pam do on her school trip?
   ☐ a. She watches TV. ☐ b. She learns about animals.

C

Listen and choose the correct picture. Then write the key word.
听一听，选择恰当的图片，并将相应的词写在下方的横线上。

1.

☐ a

☑ b

afternoon

2.

☐ a

☐ b

____

3.

☐ a

☐ b

____

4.

☐ a

☐ b

____

D Listen to *A Great Day* again. What does Pam do on most Friday afternoons? Complete the diagram.

再听一听故事，周五下午帕姆通常会做些什么？完成思维导图。

First	Next	Then	Finally
eats lunch			

E Look at D. Write. Use *First, Next, Then,* and *Finally*.

回顾上一题，用First、Next、Then和Finally写一写。

1. 

First, she eats lunch.

2. 

3. 

4. 

MY LISTENING GOALS

☐ I can listen to the story. 我能听懂这个故事。

☐ I can listen for words to understand the sequence. 我能听出表示顺序的词，理清事情发生的顺序。

UNITS **9** and **10**

Listening Check

Remember!
Listen for **times**. What do they tell you? Listen for the **sequence**. Which words show the sequence?
注意听表示时间的词，它们告诉了你什么？注意听表示顺序的词，哪些词能表明事情发生的顺序？

A Listen to the story *It's Sunday!*. What is it about? Choose the correct picture. 听一听这个故事讲了什么内容，并选择相应的图片。

A  ☐

B  ☐

C  ☐

B Which sentences show times? Choose ✔ or ✘.

哪些句子表明了时间？判断正误。

1. Jae gets up at 6:30 a.m. (✔) ✘
2. Jae eats breakfast in the morning. ✔ ✘
3. Jae walks to school at 8:00 a.m. ✔ ✘
4. Jae thinks it's a school day. ✔ ✘

C Which sentences show the sequence? Choose ✔ or ✘.

哪些句子表明了顺序？判断正误。

1. Jae is tired. He wants to sleep. ✔ (✘)
2. First, Jae gets up. ✔ ✘
3. Next, Jae gets dressed. ✔ ✘
4. Jae sees his friends at the park. ✔ ✘

D Listen to *It's Sunday!* again. Choose the correct answer.

再听一听故事，选择正确的答案。

1. What time does Jae get up?

☐ a. At 6:00 a.m. ☑ b. At 6:30 a.m. ☐ c. At 8:00 a.m.

2. What does Jae do after he eats breakfast?

☐ a. He walks to school. ☐ b. He washes his face. ☐ c. He gets dressed.

3. What does Jae do at 8:00 a.m.?

☐ a. He talks to his mom. ☐ b. He gets up. ☐ c. He walks to school.

4. Where does Jae see his friends?

☐ a. At his house. ☐ b. At the park. ☐ c. At school.

5. What happens at the end of the story?

☐ a. Jae understands it's Sunday.

☐ b. Jae has a fun day at school.

☐ c. Jae plays with his friends.

E Listen to *It's Sunday!* again. Complete the sentences.

再听一听故事，并补全句子。

The clock rings. It's 6:30 a.m. Jae is tired. He wants to sleep. It's a school day. What does Jae do in the (1) __morning__? First, Jae gets up. Next, he (2) ________ and (3) ________. Then, he eats breakfast. "Hurry up, Jae! Don't be late," says Jae's mom. Jae (4) ________ at 8:00 a.m.

He sees his friends at the park. Why aren't they at school? Oh, no! It's not a school day. It's Sunday!

UNITS 9 and 10

Get Ready to Speak

SPEAKING GOAL: Make an Appointment

口语训练目标：学会预约

An appointment is a plan to meet someone. An appointment has a time and a place. 预约是事先约定和某人见面。预约时要确定好见面时间和地点。

A **Read and listen to the appointment. Underline the time markers.** 读一读，听一听，在时间标志词下面画横线。

Speaking Tip

Use time markers, *a.m.* and *p.m.*, to tell someone when something happens.

使用a.m. 和p.m. 等时间标志词，让对方知道事情发生的具体时间。

A Doctor's Appointment

Liz: Hello? This is Doctor Park's office. Can I help you?

Eric: This is Eric Gilbert. I want to see the doctor. I feel sick. Can I make an appointment today?

Liz: There are two times open today, 10:00 a.m. or 4:30 p.m.

Eric: I can come at 4:30 p.m.

Liz: Great! See you at 4:30 p.m., Eric.

Eric: Thanks. Bye!

B **Look at A. What do you know about Eric's appointment? Complete the table.** 回顾上一题，埃里克的预约中包含哪些信息？完成表格。

Appointment	
Person	Doctor Park
Day	
Time	a.m. / p.m.
Reason	

Speak

C **Think about an appointment you want to make. Complete the table.**

制订一个预约计划，完成表格。

Appointment	
Person	
Day	
Time	a.m. / p.m.
Reason	

D **Now write about your appointment. Use your ideas from C. Choose new words, too. Then draw the person you want to see.**

顺着上一题的思路，补全预约信息，然后把你想见的人画出来。

I want to see ______________________.

Can I make an appointment on

______________________________?

I can come at ____________ a.m. / p.m.

I want to see ______________________

because ______________________.

Take turns making an appointment with your partner.

和小伙伴轮流进行预约。

MY SPEAKING GOAL

☐ **I can make an appointment.**

我会预约。

TOPIC

6

HEALTH

It's Lunchtime

MY GOALS

UNIT 11

- Listen to the radio show *Kids Tell You How*
- Listen for requests

UNIT 12

- Listen to the story *Making Lunch*
- Listen for suggestions

SPEAK

- Give a food order

A **Look at the picture. What do you see?**
看图片，回答问题。

1. What is the family doing?
2. Do you eat your food like this? When?

FUN FACT

Listen

Time to Eat!

B **Listen to the Fun Fact. Then answer the questions.** 听“奇闻趣事”，回答问题。

1. How old are chopsticks?
2. What are some chopsticks made from?

Think, Pair, Share

What food do you eat with a fork?
What food do you eat with your hands?
你用叉子吃什么食物？
你用手吃什么食物？

UNIT 11

Get Ready to Listen

A Listen, point, and say. Write the words in your picture dictionary.

听一听，指一指，说一说。在“图解词典”中写出对应的单词。

cabbage

chicken

onion

soup

B Listen and color. 听一听，涂一涂。

C Listen and write. 听一听，写一写。

1. onion
2. ______
3. ______
4. ______

Listen

LISTENING GOAL: Listen for Requests 听力训练目标：明确请求

A request is asking for something. Listen for *Can I* and *Can you* to understand what someone wants. 请求就是表达想要某物。在英语中，通常用Can I和Can you引导的一般疑问句表达请求。

A **Listen. Then complete the sentences.** 听一听，并补全句子。

1. The girl wants ___water___.
2. The boy asks for the ________.
3. The girl asks to see a ________.

Kids Tell You How

B **Listen to the radio show *Kids Tell You How*. What is it about? Choose the correct picture.**
听一听这档电台节目讲了什么内容，并选择相应的图片。

A

☐

B

☐

Now put the sentences in order. 给句子排序。

a. Amy tells Jo how to make the soup. ☐
b. Jo tries the soup. ☐
c. Amy tells Jo what she is cooking. 1

What are the **requests**?
录音中有哪些请求？

Think!
What foods do you and your family cook?
你们家通常做什么吃的？

Understand

A Think about *Kids Tell You How*. What does Jo ask for?

回想一下节目内容，乔提出了什么请求？

☐ a. She asks for soup.

☐ b. She asks for water.

Remember!
Listen for *Can I* or *Can you*. We use *Can I* and *Can you* to **request** things.
注意听Can I或者Can you引导的一般疑问句，它们通常用于提出请求。

B Listen to *Kids Tell You How* again. Choose the correct answer.

再听一听节目，圈出正确的答案。

1. Amy is making **a salad** / **(soup)**.
2. Amy's **mom** / **dad** makes this.
3. Amy **has** / **doesn't have** apples.
4. First, Amy cooks the chicken and **onions** / **rice**.
5. Amy cooks this for **12** / **20** minutes.

C Listen. Complete each sentence with a key word. Then match.

听一听，用本单元的重点词汇补全句子，并与相应的图片配对。

1. I like my mom's ___soup___ on cold days.
2. There are red ______ on the burger.
3. I don't like ______ in my salad.
4. They eat ______ sandwiches for lunch.

a. ____

b. ____

c. __1__

d. ____

D Listen to *Kids Tell You How* again. What does Amy have for the soup? Complete the table.

再听一听节目，艾米有哪些可以用来熬汤的食材？完成表格。

	Amy has	Amy doesn't have
1. onions	✔	
2. cabbage		
3. apples		
4. chicken		

E Look at D. Write. Use *have* or *don't have*.

回顾上一题，用have或don't have完成句子。

1. 

I ______have______ onions.

2. 

I ____________ cabbage.

3. 

I ____________ apples.

4. 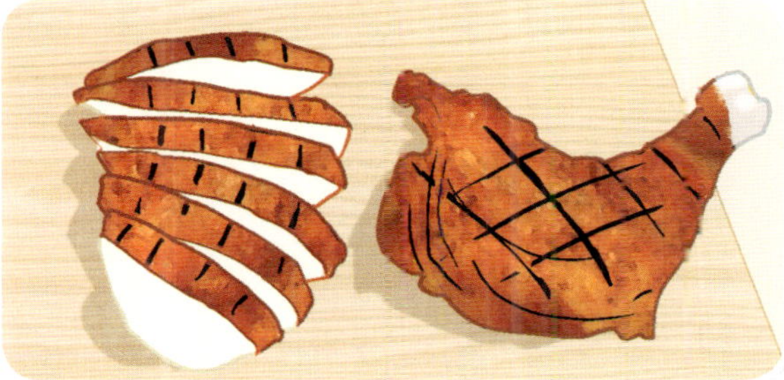

I ____________ chicken.

MY LISTENING GOALS

- ☐ I can listen to the radio show. 我能听懂这档电台节目。
- ☐ I can listen for requests to understand what someone wants. 我能听懂请求，知道讲话者想要什么。

UNIT 12

Get Ready to Listen

Let's learn the **key words.**
一起来学习重点词汇吧！

A Listen, point, and say. Write the words in your picture dictionary.

听一听，指一指，说一说。在“图解词典”中写出对应的单词。

milk

potato

sausage

sweetcorn

B Listen and number. 听一听，在圆圈里填上正确的序号。

C Listen and complete the sentences. 听一听，并补全句子。

1. My sister doesn't eat sausages .
2. I have a ______________ with my chicken.
3. Do you eat ______________ for lunch?
4. ______________ can help you sleep at night.

Listen

LISTENING GOAL: Listen for Suggestions 听力训练目标：明确建议

A suggestion is an idea about what to do. Listen for words like *Let's* to understand what someone wants to do. 建议是关于想做某事的想法。Let's 引导的祈使句通常用于提出建议。

A Listen. Choose ✓ or ✗. 听一听，并判断正误。

1. 

✓ ⓧ

2. 

✓ ✗

3. 

✓ ✗

Making Lunch

B Listen to the story *Making Lunch*. What is it about? Choose the correct picture.
听一听这个故事讲了什么内容，并选择相应的图片。

A 

B 

Now choose ✓ or ✗. 判断正误。

1. Beth and Theo are at school. ✓ ⓧ
2. There are two people in the story. ✓ ✗
3. Theo wants to cook food. ✓ ✗

What is the main **suggestion**?
录音里提了什么建议？

Think!
What foods do you like? Why?
你喜欢吃什么？为什么？

Understand

Remember!
Listen for the **suggestion** words. Words like *Let's* show you what someone wants to do.
注意听表示建议的词。Let's 引导的祈使句通常用于提出建议。

A Think about *Making Lunch*.
What does Beth suggest? Choose Yes or No.

回想一下故事，贝丝提了什么建议？判断正误。

1. Let's watch TV. **Yes** **No**
2. Let's make lunch. **Yes** **No**

B Listen to *Making Lunch* again. Choose the correct answer.

再听一听故事，选择正确的答案。

1. Where are Beth and Theo?
   - [ ] a. At school.
   - [x] b. At home.
2. What food does Beth ask Theo about first?
   - [ ] a. Potatoes.
   - [ ] b. Sausages.
3. What does Theo want to drink?
   - [ ] a. Water.
   - [ ] b. Milk.

C Listen and choose the correct picture. Then write the key word.

听一听，选择恰当的图片，并将相应的词写在下方的横线上。

1.

[ ] a

[x] b

sweetcorn

2.

[ ] a

[ ] b

____

3.

[ ] a

[ ] b

____

4.

[ ] a

[ ] b

____

D Listen to *Making Lunch* again. What does Theo want? Complete the diagram. Work with a partner.

再听一听故事，西奥想要什么？和小伙伴一起完成思维导图。

Theo

wants	doesn't want
________	potatoes
________	________
________	________

E Look at D. Write. Use *wants* or *doesn't want*.

回顾上一题，用wants或doesn't want完成句子。

1. 

He doesn't want potatoes.

2. 

He ________________ ________________.

3. 

He ________________ ________________.

4. 

He ________________ ________________.

MY LISTENING GOALS

- [ ] I can listen to the story. 我能听懂这个故事。
- [ ] I can listen for suggestions to know what someone wants to do. 我能听懂表示建议的话，知道别人想做什么。

UNITS 11 and 12

Listening Check

Remember!
Listen for **requests**. What do people ask for? Listen for **suggestions**. What do people want to do?
注意听请求，人们想要什么？注意听建议，人们想做什么？

A Listen to the story *From the Farm*. What is it about? Choose the correct picture.

听一听这个故事讲了什么内容，并选择相应的图片。

A

B

C

B What is the request? Choose ✔ or ✘.

故事里提了什么请求？判断一下。

1. We have cabbage. ✔ ✘
2. Can I try the sweetcorn? ✔ ✘
3. Let's eat! ✔ ✘
4. We have onions. ✔ ✘

C What is the suggestion? Choose ✔ or ✘.

故事里提了什么建议？判断一下。

1. We have potatoes. ✔ ✘
2. Our corn is great! ✔ ✘
3. Can I try the sweetcorn? ✔ ✘
4. Let's eat! ✔ ✘

D Listen to *From the Farm* again. Choose the correct answer.

再听一听故事，选择正确的答案。

1. Where does Jill visit Zoe?
   - ☐ a. At school.
   - ☑ b. At Zoe's house.
   - ☐ c. At Jill's house.
2. Where does Zoe live?
   - ☐ a. On a farm.
   - ☐ b. In a city.
   - ☐ c. Near school.
3. What does Zoe's family do?
   - ☐ a. Cut hair.
   - ☐ b. Grow food.
   - ☐ c. Paint houses.
4. What does Jill ask Zoe?
   - ☐ a. To try food.
   - ☐ b. To cook food.
   - ☐ c. To buy food.
5. What does Zoe suggest?
   - ☐ a. Let's cook food.
   - ☐ b. Let's play a game.
   - ☐ c. Let's eat the food.

E Listen to *From the Farm* again. Complete the sentences.

再听一听故事，并补全句子。

Jill goes on a trip. She visits her friend, Zoe. Zoe is eight years old. She lives in a small town. Zoe's family has a farm. They grow food. "We have (1) __cabbage__. We have (2) ________. We have (3) ________. And we have (4) ________," Zoe says. "Can I try the sweetcorn?" Jill asks Zoe. "Yes, you can," Zoe says. "Our corn is great! Let's eat!"

Zoe is very happy. She likes her farm. Jill likes Zoe's farm, too.

UNITS 11 and 12

Get Ready to Speak

SPEAKING GOAL: Give a Food Order 口语训练目标：点菜

An order is a request for food in a restaurant or café. You tell your order to the server. Then, you eat!
点菜就是在饭店或者便餐馆里把自己想要的食物告诉服务员，等上菜了就可以吃啦！

A **Read and listen to the order. Underline *please* and *thank you*.**
读一读，听一听，在please和thank you下面画横线。

Speaking Tip
Use words like *please* and *thank you* when you give a food order.
点菜时要说please和thank you。

Today's Specials

Sue: Can I take your order?
Eric: I want the chicken soup, please.
Sue: OK, great. Do you want anything else?
Eric: Yes, I do. Can I have water, please?
Sue: Sure. Thank you for your order.
Eric: Thank you.

B **Look at A. What are the replies to the questions? Complete the diagram.**
回顾上一题，问题都得到了什么样的回答？完成思维导图。

Questions		Replies
1. Can I take your order?	→	I want the chicken soup, please.
2. Do you want anything else?	→	Yes, ________________.
3. Can I have water, please?	→	____________. Thank you for your order.

Speak

C **Think about the food you want to eat in restaurant. Answer the questions. Complete the diagram.** 想一想，你在饭店里想点什么菜？回答问题，并完成思维导图。

Questions		Replies
Can I take your order?	→	
Do you want anything else?	→	
Can I have water, please?	→	

D **Now write your order. Use your ideas from C. Choose new words, too. Then draw your food.**
顺着上一题的思路，把你要点的菜写下来，然后把你想吃的东西画出来。

Today's Specials

____

____

Do you want anything else?

____

____

What do you want to eat? Give and take a food order with your partner.
你想吃什么呢？和小伙伴一起试着用英语点菜吧。

MY SPEAKING GOAL

☐ **I can give and take a food order.**
我会点菜，也会提供点菜服务。

Listening WITH Speaking 2

Workbook

WORKBOOK

UNIT

1

Listen

LISTENING GOAL:

Listen for the Main Idea

听力训练目标：明确主旨

Remember!

The **main idea** gives more information about the topic. It's in the first sentence.

主旨提供了更多与话题有关的信息。通常第一句话就是主旨句。

A Listen to the passage *Friendly Faces*. Then put the pictures in order.

听一听这篇文章，给图片排序。

A

☐

B

☐

C

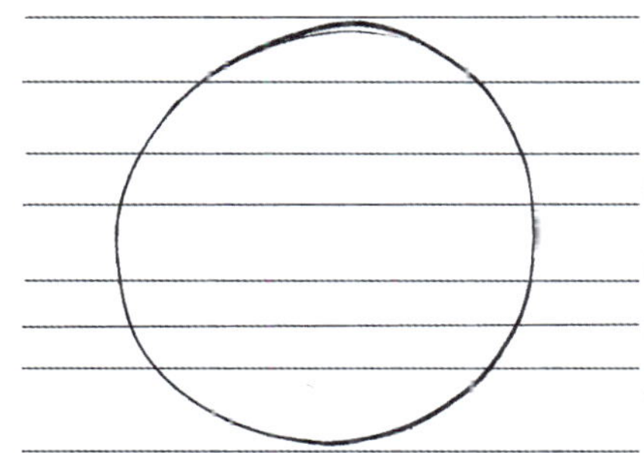

1

B Think about *Friendly Faces*. What is the main idea? Choose ✔ or ✘.

回想一下文章，它的主旨是什么？判断正误。

1. Making art at school. ✔ ✘
2. How to draw a face. ✔ ✘
3. How to draw with a pencil. ✔ ✘

C Listen to *Friendly Faces* again. Choose the correct answer.

再听一听文章，选择正确的答案。

1. What shape does she draw?

   ☐ a. A circle. ☑ b. An oval. ☐ c. A square.

2. What does she use to draw the lines?

   ☐ a. A ruler. ☐ b. Stickers. ☐ c. A crayon.

3. What do you draw first?

   ☐ a. Nose. ☐ b. Eyes. ☐ c. Mouth.

4. What does the girl do last?

   ☐ a. She draws Tom. ☐ b. She draws the hair. ☐ c. She colors the face.

D Listen and write the word. Then choose the correct picture.

听一听，写出正确的单词，并选择相应的图片。

1. drawing

☐ a

☑ b

2. ______

☐ a

☐ b

3. ______

☐ a

☐ b

4. ______

☐ a

☐ b

E Complete the sentences. 选一选，填一填。

classmates	chairs	~~decorations~~	drawing	bookcase	stickers

1. We are making decorations for the party.
2. Eddie and Tina are ______.
3. I'm putting the ______ on my book.
4. I use a pencil to make a ______.

F Unscramble and write. 理一理，写出正确的单词。

1. t s k i c e r

   sticker

2. o e d c t r a s i o n

   ______

3. l c a s m s a s t e

   ______

4. a d r g w i n

   ______

WORKBOOK

UNIT

2

Listen

LISTENING GOAL: Listen for Details

听力训练目标：捕捉细节

Remember!

A **detail** is a word or sentence about the main idea. Details tell you more information about the main idea.

细节可以是一个单词，也可能是一个句子。细节有助于你了解主旨。

A Listen to the conversation *School Visit*. What do you hear about? Choose ✔ or ✘.

听一听这段对话，你听到了什么内容？判断正误。

1. 

A coat hook. ✔ ✘

2. 

A poster. ✔ ✘

B Think about *School Visit*. What are the details? Choose ✔ or ✘.

回想一下对话，里面有哪些细节？判断正误。

1. Ada meets Noah's classmates. ✔ ✘
2. Ada visits Noah's classroom. ✔ ✘
3. Noah shows Ada some drawings. ✔ ✘

C Listen to *School Visit* again. Choose Yes or No.

再听一听对话，判断正误。

1. Ada is Noah's sister. Yes No
2. Noah shows Ada his desk. Yes No
3. Noah's desk is next to the window. Yes No
4. Noah shows Ada a mouse named Fred. Yes No
5. There is a poster about turtles. Yes No
6. Ada goes to school next year. Yes No

D Listen. Then read and choose the correct answer.

听一听，读一读，并选择正确的答案。

1. What is by the classroom door?

(a.) 

b. 

c. 

2. What is on the bookcase?

a. 

b. 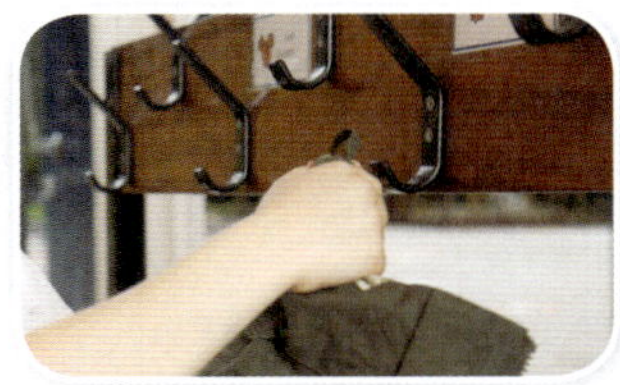

c. 

3. What is Sue making?

a. 

b. 

c. 

E Complete the missing words. 根据首字母提示，用本单元的重点词汇补全句子。

1. We put drawings on the wall of our classroom________.
2. I can find our country on the g____________.
3. I hang my backpack on my c________ h________.
4. My p____________ has pictures of turtles on it.

Speak

Remember!
A request is a question. You start a request with the word *can*.
你可以用can引导的疑问句来提出请求。

Circle the word *can* in the sentences.
Then think of your own requests. Tell your partner.

把疑问句中的can圈出来，然后试着向小伙伴提出一些请求。

Can you pass me the stickers?

Can I have a pencil?

WORKBOOK

UNIT 3

Listen

LISTENING GOAL: Listen for Action Words

听力训练目标：听清行为动词

Remember!
Words like *run*, *jump*, and *swing* are **action words**. They tell you what people are doing in a story.
行为动词就是表示动作的词，例如run、jump和swing就是行为动词。这类词告诉你故事中的人正在做什么。

A Listen to the story ***Don't Sleep!***. Then put the pictures in order.
听一听这个故事，给图片排序。

A ☐ B ☐ C ☐

B Think about ***Don't Sleep!***. Which sentences have action words? Choose ✔ or ✘. 回想一下故事，下列句子中有行为动词吗？判断正误。

1. Rabbit can run. ☑ ✔ ☐ ✘
2. Turtle is very slow. ☐ ✔ ☐ ✘
3. Turtle can walk. ☐ ✔ ☐ ✘

C Listen to ***Don't Sleep!*** again. Choose the correct answer.
再听一听故事，选择正确的答案。

1. Who are running a race?
   ☐ a. Rabbit and Cat. ☑ b. Rabbit and Turtle. ☐ c. Dog and Cat.
2. What can't Turtle do?
   ☐ a. Win. ☐ b. Run. ☐ c. Walk.
3. What does Rabbit do?
   ☐ a. She walks. ☐ b. She wins the race. ☐ c. She sleeps.
4. What does Turtle do?
   ☐ a. He wins the race. ☐ b. He runs. ☐ c. He sleeps.

D Listen and write the word. Then choose the correct picture.

听一听，写出正确的单词，并选择相应的图片。

1. ______run______

☑ a

☐ b

2. ______________

☐ a

☐ b

3. ______________

☐ a

☐ b

4. ______________

☐ a

☐ b

E Complete the sentences. 选一选，填一填。

dance	~~jump~~	run	skip	swing	walk

1. I like to ___jump___ in the pool with my friends.
2. We ______________ to our classroom at school. We don't run.
3. We ______________ fast in the race. We don't walk.
4. The monkey likes to ______________ from trees.

F Unscramble and write. 理一理，写出正确的单词。

1. w s i g n

   ______swing______

2. k w a l

   ____

3. p j u m

   ____

4. r n u

   ____

WORKBOOK

UNIT 4

Listen

LISTENING GOAL:
Listen for Gist
听力训练目标：把握大意

Remember!
The **gist** is what a passage is mostly about. Look at the pictures, title, and questions.
大意是听力材料的主要内容。图片、标题和问题能给我们一些提示。

A Listen to the passage *Bella Learns New Things*. What is it about? Choose ✔ or ✘.

听一听这篇文章讲了什么内容，并判断正误。

1. 

Jo's friends. ✔ ✘

2. 

Jo's hobby. ✔ ✘

B Think about *Bella Learns New Things*. What is the gist? Choose ✔ or ✘.

回想一下文章，它的大意是什么？判断正误。

1. Jo has a dog as a pet. ✔ (✘)
2. Jo teaches her dog new things. ✔ ✘
3. Jo walks her dog every day. ✔ ✘

C Listen to *Bella Learns New Things* again. Choose Yes or No.

再听一听文章，判断正误。

1. Bella is Jo's dog. (Yes) No
2. Bella can't hop. Yes No
3. Bella likes to dance. Yes No
4. Jo and Bella can't dance. Yes No
5. Bella can jump over Jo. Yes No
6. Bella is smart. Yes No

D Listen. Then read and choose the correct answer.

听一听，读一读，并选择正确的答案。

1. What can Carlos do?

a. 

(b.) 

c. 

2. What does Lucy like to do?

a. 

b. 

c. 

3. What can you do in the gym at school?

a. 

b. 

c. 

E Complete the missing words. 根据首字母提示，用本单元的重点词汇补全句子。

1. David can rollerblade ________ fast.
2. My h________ is dancing.
3. I like playing s________ with my friends.
4. I can h________ on one foot.

Remember!
Use time phrases like *every Monday, Wednesday to Friday*, and *on the weekend* to show when.
用表示时间的短语，比如 every Monday、Wednesday to Friday或者 on the weekend表明时间。

Speak

Circle the time phrases in the sentences.
Then think of other time phrases. Tell your partner.

把表示时间的短语圈出来，然后想一想还有哪些短语能表示时间，和小伙伴说一说。

I play soccer every Wednesday.

From Monday to Friday, I go to school.

I ride my bike on the weekend.

WORKBOOK

UNIT

5

Listen

LISTENING GOAL:
Listen for Prices
听力训练目标：明确价格

Remember!
Price words, like dollars and cents, tell you how much something is.
像dollars和cents这样的货币单位能给你价格提示。

A Listen to the conversation *Cool Clothes*. What do you hear about? Choose ✓ or ✗. 听一听这段对话，你听到了什么内容？判断正误。

1. 

School. ✓ ✗

2. 

Shopping. ✓ ✗

B Think about *Cool Clothes*. Are the price words correct? Choose ✓ or ✗.
回想一下对话，下列句子中的价格正确吗？判断正误。

1. The T-shirt is 50 dollars. ✓ ✗
2. The T-shirt is 30 dollars. ✓ ✗
3. Jill buys some clothes for 20 dollars. ✓ ✗

C Listen to *Cool Clothes* again. Choose the correct answer.
再听一听对话，选择正确的答案。

1. Who do Jill and Lucy see at the mall?
   - ☐ a. Jill's sister.
   - ☐ b. Their friend.
   - ☑ c. An older girl.
2. What does Mei have?
   - ☐ a. A smartphone.
   - ☐ b. A watch.
   - ☐ c. Some candy.
3. What does Lucy want to buy?
   - ☐ a. A T-shirt.
   - ☐ b. Some candy.
   - ☐ c. A smartphone.
4. What does Mei like?
   - ☐ a. Lucy's watch.
   - ☐ b. Jill and Lucy's T-shirts.
   - ☐ c. Jill and Lucy's smartphones.

D Listen and write the word. Then choose the correct picture.

听一听，写出正确的单词，并选择相应的图片。

1. smartphone

☐ a

☑ b

2. ______

☐ a

☐ b

3. ______

☐ a

☐ b

4. ______

☐ a

☐ b

E Complete the sentences. 选一选，填一填。

~~clothes~~	comic book	smartphone	T-shirt	vase	watch

1. Your sister wears cool clothes.
2. My friend and I put the flowers in a nice ______.
3. I wear a ______ and jeans to school.
4. I call my mom on my ______.

F Unscramble and write. 理一理，写出正确的单词。

1. T - t h s i r

   T-shirt

2. s v e a

   ______

3. l c o t s h e

   ______

4. m t a r p e s h o n

   ______

WORKBOOK

UNIT 6

Listen

LISTENING GOAL:
Listen for Days of the Week
听力训练目标：听清是星期几

Remember!
Days tell you when something happens. *Monday* is a day.
像Monday这样的词是英文中表示星期几的词，这类词能告诉你事情发生的时间。

A Listen to the story *A Trip to Tokyo*. Then put the pictures in order.
听一听这个故事，给图片排序。

B Think about *A Trip to Tokyo*. Which days do you hear? Choose ✔ or ✘.
回想一下故事，你听到了哪些日期？判断正误。

1. It is Saturday today. ✔ ✘
2. Phil goes home on Monday. ✔ ✘
3. Yuto goes shopping on Wednesday. ✔ ✘

C Listen to *A Trip to Tokyo* again. Choose Yes or No.
再听一听故事，判断正误。

1. Phil lives in Tokyo. **Yes** **No**
2. Phil and Yuto go to a mall. **Yes** **No**
3. Phil is with his brother. **Yes** **No**
4. Phil has 40 dollars. **Yes** **No**
5. Phil's brother doesn't have a camera. **Yes** **No**
6. Yuto and Phil look for some clothes. **Yes** **No**

D Listen. Then read and choose the correct answer.

听一听，读一读，并选择正确的答案。

1. What toy does Tom buy?

a. 
b. 
c. 

2. What does Kim have?

a. 
b. 
c. 

3. What do they put in the shopping cart?

a. 
b. 
c. 

E Complete the missing words. 根据首字母提示，用本单元的重点词汇补全句子。

1. There are many shopping carts at the store.
2. I take pictures with my c__________.
3. My younger brother has a lot of t__________.
4. I like your toy p__________.

Speak

Remember!
Use questions like *What about you?* to exchange information.
用问句，比如What about you？来询问关于某人的信息。

Circle the sentences that exchange information. Then think of your own sentences. Tell your partner.

把表示交换信息的句子圈出来，然后自己想一些类似的句子，和小伙伴说一说。

I like T-shirts. What about you?

My favorite store is the toy store. What is your favorite store?

WORKBOOK

UNIT 7

Listen

LISTENING GOAL: Listen for Places

听力训练目标：听清地点

Remember!
A **place** tells you where people are. Places are countries, cities, and buildings.
地点可以是具体的国家、城市或者建筑物，它们能告诉你人们在哪里。

A Listen to the conversation ***My Favorite Job***. What do you hear about? Choose ✔ or ✘. 听一听这段对话，你听到了什么内容？判断正误。

1. 

A zookeeper. ✔ ✘

2. 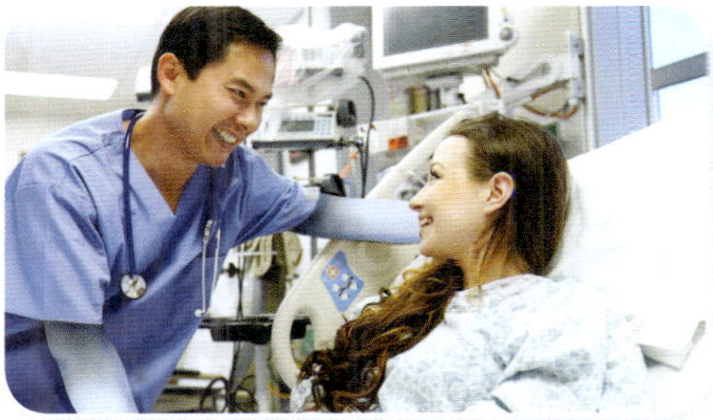

A nurse. ✔ ✘

B Think about ***My Favorite Job***. Are these places in the conversation? Choose ✔ or ✘. 回想一下对话，里面提到下列地点了吗？判断正误。

1. Restaurant. ✔ ✘
2. New York City. ✔ ✘
3. Home. ✔ ✘

C Listen to ***My Favorite Job*** again. Choose the correct answer.
再听一听对话，选择正确的答案。

1. What does May show Li?
   ☐ a. A picture. ☐ b. A drawing. ☐ c. A book.
2. What doesn't Li like?
   ☐ a. Restaurants. ☐ b. Cooking. ☐ c. Hot weather.
3. Who is in Li's picture?
   ☐ a. A nurse. ☐ b. A painter. ☐ c. A zookeeper.
4. What job do they choose for their project?
   ☐ a. A zookeeper. ☐ b. A chef. ☐ c. A barber.

D Listen and write the word. Then choose the correct picture.

听一听，写出正确的单词，并选择相应的图片。

1. nurse

☐ a

☑ b

2. ______

☐ a

☐ b

3. ______

☐ a

☐ b

4. ______

☐ a

☐ b

E Complete the sentences. 选一选，填一填。

barber	~~chef~~	nurse	painter	server	zookeeper

1. Dan is a chef. He cooks food in a restaurant.
2. The ______ works with animals.
3. A ______ helps sick people.
4. Colors are important for a ______.

F Unscramble and write. 理一理，写出正确的单词。

1. a i r n p t e

painter

2. f c h e

______

3. z o e o k e r p e

______

4. u n r e s

______

WORKBOOK

UNIT

8

Listen

LISTENING GOAL: Listen for Addresses

听力训练目标：听清地址

Remember!
An **address** tells you where people live or work. An address has a number and street name.
地址能告诉你人们在哪里居住或工作，地址包括街道名称和编号。

A Listen to the story *The Wrong Address*. Then put the pictures in order.

听一听这个故事，给图片排序。

A

☐

B

☐

C

☐

B Think about *The Wrong Address*. Which is the correct address? Choose ✔ or ✘.

回想一下故事，下列哪个地址是正确的？判断正误。

1. The library is at 455 Park Street. ✔ (✘)
2. Mrs. Chen works at 455 Park Street. ✔ ✘
3. Mr. Lee works at 455 Park Street. ✔ ✘

C Listen to *The Wrong Address* again. Choose Yes or No.

再听一听故事，判断正误。

1. The box is for Mrs. Chen. **Yes** **(No)**
2. Mrs. Chen is at the library. **Yes** **No**
3. Eli takes the box to the right address. **Yes** **No**
4. Mr. Lee is the librarian. **Yes** **No**
5. Mrs. Chen has Mr. Lee's box. **Yes** **No**
6. Mrs. Chen is Mr. Lee's sister. **Yes** **No**

D Listen. Then read and choose the correct answer.

听一听，读一读，并选择正确的答案。

1. Who helps Tom?

a. 

(b.) 

c. 

2. Who puts things on tables?

a. 

b. 

c. 

3. Who is working?

a. 

b. 

c. 

E Complete the missing words. 根据首字母提示，用本单元的重点词汇补全句子。

1. The barber__________ can cut my hair.
2. The p__________ w__________ puts mail in our mail box.
3. The s__________ works in the restaurant.
4. The l__________ reads books to us at school.

Speak

Remember!
Use location words like *in*, *at*, and *on* to help you describe where something is.
使用in、at、on等方位词有助于你描述事物的具体位置。

Circle *in*, *at*, or *on* and a place in each sentence. Then think of your own sentences with *in*, *at*, or *on*. Tell your partner.

把句子中的 in、at、on，以及地点圈出来，然后想一些带有这些方位词的句子，和小伙伴说一说。

The library is on Park Street.

My mom works at a small restaurant.

WORKBOOK

UNIT

9

Listen

LISTENING GOAL:

Listen for Times

听力训练目标：明确时间

Remember!

Listen for **times**. Times tell you when things happen.

注意听表示时间的词，它们能告诉你事情发生的具体时间。

A Listen to the passage *Time for School*. What do you hear about? Choose ✔ or ✘.

听一听这篇文章，你听到了什么内容？判断正误。

1. 

A favorite sport. ☐✔ ☐✘

2. 

A walk to school. ☐✔ ☐✘

B Think about *Time for School*. Which sentences show the times? Choose ✔ or ✘.

回想一下文章，下列句子中有时间状语吗？判断正误。

1. Ali gets up at 6:00 a.m. ☐✔ ☐✘
2. Ali eats his breakfast. ☐✔ ☐✘
3. Ali walks to school at 8:00 a.m. ☐✔ ☐✘

C Listen to *Time for School* again. Choose the correct answer.

再听一听文章，选择正确的答案。

1. What does Ali do after he gets up in the morning?
   ☑ a. He washes his face. ☐ b. He eats breakfast. ☐ c. He plays.
2. What does Ali do at 8:00 a.m.?
   ☐ a. He eats breakfast. ☐ b. He walks to school. ☐ c. He gets dressed.
3. Who does Ali walk to school with?
   ☐ a. His brother. ☐ b. His mom. ☐ c. His friends.
4. What does Ali cross on his way to school?
   ☐ a. Water. ☐ b. A park. ☐ c. A road.

D Listen and write the word. Then choose the correct picture.

听一听，写出正确的单词或短语，并选择相应的图片。

1. wash my face

☐ a

☑ b

2. ________

☐ a

☐ b

3. ________

☐ a

☐ b

4. ________

☐ a

☐ b

E Complete the sentences. 选一选，填一填。

do homework	~~get dressed~~	morning	walk to school	wash my face	watch TV

1. I get dressed at 7:30 a.m. I wear jeans and a T-shirt.
2. I eat breakfast in the ________.
3. I get up at 6:00 a.m. and ________ with water.
4. I ________ with my friends. I don't ride the bus.

F Unscramble and write. 理一理，写出正确的单词或短语。

1. w k a l o t c s h o l o

walk to school

2. s w h a y m c f a e

____

3. o m r g n i n

____

4. g t e r d e s d s e

____

WORKBOOK

UNIT

10

Listen

LISTENING GOAL:
Listen for Sequence
听力训练目标：理清顺序

Remember!
Listen to the **sequence words**. The sequence words tell you the order things happen.
注意听表示顺序的词，它们能告诉你事情发生的顺序。

A Listen to the story *It's Bedtime!*. Then put the pictures in order.

听一听这个故事，给图片排序。

A

☐

B

☐

C

☐

B Think about *It's Bedtime!*. What sequence words are in the story? Choose ✔ or ✘.

回想一下故事，里面出现了哪些表示顺序的词？判断正误。

1. First, Jill watches TV. ✔ ✘
2. Jill reads her book. ✔ ✘
3. Finally, Jill goes to sleep at 7:00 p.m. ✔ ✘

C Listen to *It's Bedtime!* again. Choose Yes or No.

再听一听故事，判断正误。

1. Jill goes to bed early in the evening. Yes No
2. Jill watches TV and reads in the evening. Yes No
3. Jill is very sleepy at school the next day. Yes No
4. Jill and her dad play games in the afternoon. Yes No
5. Jill doesn't watch TV the next night. Yes No
6. Jill goes to sleep at 7:00 p.m. the next evening. Yes No

D Listen. Then read and choose the correct answer.

听一听，读一读，并选择正确的答案。

1. What does Tom do in the afternoon?

(a.) 
b. 
c. 

2. When does Emily read with her mom?

a. 
b. 
c. 

3. What does Sam do at 8:00 p.m.?

a. 
b. 
c. 

E Complete the missing words. 根据首字母提示，用本单元的重点词汇补全句子。

1. I go to sleep ________ at 9:00 p.m. on Saturdays.
2. We eat lunch at 1:00 in the a________.
3. I have a busy d________ at school today.
4. My brother does his homework in the e________.

Remember!
Use time markers, like *a.m.* and *p.m.*, to tell someone when something happens.
使用a.m.和p.m.等时间标志词，让对方知道事情发生的具体时间。

Speak

Circle the time markers in the sentences. Then think of your own sentence with a time marker. Tell your partner.

把句子中的时间标志词圈出来，然后试着用这些词造句，和小伙伴说一说。

My art class is at 11:00 a.m. on Tuesday.

I get up at 7:00 in the morning.

WORKBOOK

UNIT

11

Listen

LISTENING GOAL: Listen for Requests

听力训练目标：明确请求

Remember!
A **request** is asking for something. Use *Can I* and *Can you* to request things.
请求就是表达想要某物。在英语中通常用Can I和Can you引导的一般疑问句表达请求。

A Listen to the show ***Onion Day***. What do you hear about? Choose ✔ or ✘. 听一听这档节目，你听到了什么内容？判断正误。

1.

Fruit. ☐ ✔ ☐ ✘

2.

A market. ☐ ✔ ☐ ✘

B Think about ***Onion Day***. Which is the request? Choose ✔ or ✘.
回想一下节目内容，下列哪个句子是表达请求的？判断正误。

1. Do you like cabbage? ☐ ✔ ☐ ✘ (circled)
2. Can I try this onion soup, Chef? ☐ ✔ ☐ ✘
3. The onion soup is great! ☐ ✔ ☐ ✘

C Listen to ***Onion Day*** again. Choose the correct answer.
再听一听节目，选择正确的答案。

1. Where is Mia?
   ☑ a. At a market. ☐ b. At school. ☐ c. At a restaurant.
2. Who does Mia talk to?
   ☐ a. Her friend. ☐ b. A barber. ☐ c. A chef.
3. What is the main food Mia talks about?
   ☐ a. Cheese. ☐ b. Soup. ☐ c. Pizza.
4. What food does Mia eat?
   ☐ a. Sweetcorn. ☐ b. Pizza. ☐ c. Onion soup.

D Listen and write the word. Then choose the correct picture.

听一听，写出正确的单词，并选择相应的图片。

1. soup

☑ a

☐ b

2. ______

☐ a

☐ b

3. ______

☐ a

☐ b

4. ______

☐ a

☐ b

E Complete the sentences. 选一选，填一填。

~~cabbage~~	chicken	pizza	onions	salad	soup

1. Ryoko cuts some cabbage and onions for her salad.
2. You eat ______ with a spoon. You can't eat it with a fork!
3. These ______ have a bad smell.
4. I don't feel good, so I'm eating ______ soup.

F Unscramble and write. 理一理，写出正确的单词。

1. n o o i n

onion

2. b c a e b a g

______

3. s p o u

______

4. c i c n k e h

______

WORKBOOK
UNIT
12

Listen

LISTENING GOAL: Listen for Suggestions

听力训练目标：明确建议

Remember!
Listen for **suggestions** with *Let's* to understand what someone wants to do.
Let's 引导的祈使句通常用于提出建议。

A Listen to the story *New Food*. Then put the pictures in order.

听一听这个故事，给图片排序。

A

☐

B

☐

C

☐

B Think about *New Food*. Which is the suggestion? Choose ✔ or ✘.

回想一下故事，下列哪个句子是建议？判断正误。

1. Lee and Onur eat lunch. ✔ ✘
2. Let's eat. ✔ ✘
3. Drink this water! ✔ ✘

C Listen to *New Food* again. Choose Yes or No.

再听一听故事，判断正误。

1. Lee is at his friend's house. Yes No
2. Onur suggests they eat at a restaurant. Yes No
3. There is a lot of food on the table. Yes No
4. Lee thinks the sausage is hot. Yes No
5. Onur tells Lee to drink water. Yes No
6. Lee doesn't like the food at Onur's home. Yes No

D Listen. Then read and choose the correct answer.

听一听，读一读，并选择正确的答案。

1. What does Ruby want?

a. 

(b.) 

c. 

2. What does Anna eat for lunch?

a. 

b. 

c. 

3. What does Bill like on pizza?

a. 

b. 

c. 

E Complete the missing words. 根据首字母提示，用本单元的重点词汇补全句子。

1. My dad eats one potato__________ every day.
2. I drink m__________ for breakfast.
3. There is s__________ in the salad.
4. Mom cooks s__________ and potatoes for lunch.

Remember!
Use words like *please* and *thank you* when you give a food order.
点菜时要说please和thank you。

Speak

Circle *please* and *thank you* in the sentences.
Then think of your own sentences. Tell your partner.

把句子中的 please 和 thank you 圈出来，然后试着用这些词造句，和小伙伴说一说。

Can I have milk, please?

Thank you, but I don't want potatoes.

Picture Dictionary

Write the key words.
写出重点词汇。

Unit 1

Unit 2

Unit 3

Unit 4

Unit 5

Unit 6

Unit 7

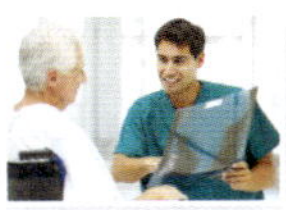

Unit 8

Unit 9

Unit 10

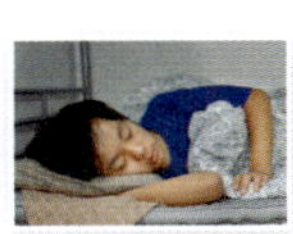

Unit 11

Unit 12

Answer Key

pp6–7

A
1. Answers will vary.
2. Answers will vary.

B
1. The school is on the river.
2. Answers will vary.

p8

B
Students color the class-mates' chairs red.
Students color the decorations blue.
Students color the drawing yellow.
Students color the sticker green.

C
1. decorations
2. sticker
3. classmates
4. drawing

p9

A
1. cat
2. classmate
3. school

B
A
a. 3
b. 2
c. 1

pp10–11

A
a

B
1. at school
2. flowers
3. orange
4. dinosaur
5. a drawing

C
1. classmates, b
2. decorations, a
3. stickers, d
4. drawing, c

D
1. drawing
2. pencil
3. decorations
4. stickers

E
1. that
2. Those
3. That
4. those

p12

B
1. globe
2. poster
3. classroom
4. coat hooks

C
1. poster
2. globe
3. classroom
4. coat hook

p13

A
1. ✓
2. ×
3. ✓

B
B
1. ×
2. ×
3. ✓

pp14–15

A
1. Yes
2. No

B
1. b
2. b
3. a

C
1. a, classroom
2. b, coat hooks
3. a, globe
4. b, poster

D
1. Is it a globe? / Yes, it is.
2. Are they / Yes, they are.
3. Is it / Yes, it is.
4. Is it / Yes, it is.

E
1. Is it / Yes, it is.
2. Are they / Yes, they are.
3. Is it / Yes, it is.
4. Is it / Yes, it is.

pp16–17

A
B

B
1. ×
2. ✓
3. ✓
4. ×

C
1. ×
2. ✓
3. ×
4. ✓

D
1. b
2. a
3. c
4. b
5. a

E
(1) classmates
(2) decorations
(3) poster
(4) drawing

pp18–19

A
Underline:
Can I have some crayons?
Can you give me the red and green crayons, please?

B
1. have some crayons
2. give me the red and green crayons

C
Answers will vary.

D
Answers will vary.

pp20–21

A
1. Answers will vary.
2. Answers will vary.

B
1. You go inside a big, round ball and move.
2. Answers will vary.

p22

B
Students color the jumping girl's shirt green.
Students color the swinging boy's cap red.
Students color the running boy's shoes blue.
Students color the walking girl's skirt yellow.

C

1. swing
2. jump
3. walk
4. run

p23

A

1. runs
2. walks
3. jumps

B

B

a. 2
b. 1
c. 3

pp24–25

A

a

B

1. games
2. men
3. run
4. jump
5. can't

C

1. walk, d
2. runs, b
3. jump, a
4. swing, c

D

1. Can she
2. Can they
3. Can he
4. Can he/she

E

1. Can she see?
2. Can they run?
3. Can he jump?
4. Can she swing?

p26

B

1. dance
2. basketball
3. rollerblade
4. hopscotch

C

1. hop
2. rollerblade
3. hobby
4. sports

p27

A

1. ✓
2. ×
3. ✓

B

B

1. ✓
2. ×
3. ×

pp28–29

A

1. No
2. Yes

B

1. b
2. a
3. b

C

1. a, rollerblade
2. b, hop
3. a, hobby
4. b, sports

D

1. to rollerblade
2. to go fast
3. to go slow
4. to walk

E

1. Yes, she does.
2. No, she doesn't.
3. Yes, she does.
4. No, she doesn't.

pp30–31

A

C

B

1. ✓
2. ×
3. ✓
4. ×

C

1. ×
2. ✓
3. ×
4. ✓

D

1. c
2. b
3. c
4. a
5. b

E

(1) sports
(2) run
(3) jump
(4) rollerblade

pp32–33

A

Underline: every Monday, From Wednesday to Friday, in the mornings, on the weekend

B

1. do karate
2. run in the mornings
3. don't play sports, walk with friends, ride bike, sleep a lot

C

Answers will vary.

D

Answers will vary.

pp34–35

A

1. Answers will vary.
2. Answers will vary.

B

1. It's a market.
2. Answers will vary.

p36

B

Students color the smartphone purple.

Students color the vase orange.

Students color the T-shirt blue.

Students color the clothes green.

C

1. clothes
2. smartphone
3. vase
4. T-shirt

p37

A

1. a
2. b
3. a

B

B

a. 2
b. 3
c. 1

pp38–39

A

a

B

1. market
2. father
3. hair
4. dollars
5. small

C

1. clothes, c
2. smartphone, d
3. T-shirts, a
4. vases, b

D

1. Yes
2. Yes
3. Yes
4. No

E

1. Yes, she does.
2. Yes, she does.
3. Yes, she does.
4. No, she doesn't.

p40

B
1. toy robots
2. camera
3. toy planes
4. shopping cart

C
1. toys
2. shopping cart
3. camera
4. plane

p41

A
1. Sunday
2. Friday
3. Wednesday

B
A
1. ✓
2. ×
3. ×

pp42–43

A
1. Yes
2. No

B
1. a
2. b
3. a

C
1. a, plane
2. a, shopping cart
3. b, toy
4. b, camera

D
1. camera store
2. toy store
3. art store
4. ice cream store

E
1. They're
2. They're
3. It's
4. It's

pp44–45

A
C

B
1. ✓
2. ×
3. ✓
4. ×

C
1. ✓
2. ×
3. ✓
4. ×

D
1. b
2. c
3. a
4. c
5. b

E
(1) toys
(2) clothes
(3) T-shirt
(4) candy

pp46–47

A
Underline:
What's your favorite store?
What about you?
What's your favorite store?

B
Kim: toy store, scooters
Tom: clothes store, T-shirts

C
Answers will vary.

D
Answers will vary.

pp48–49

A
1. Answers will vary.
2. Answers will vary.

B
1. He travels all around the world to take photos of animals.
2. Answers will vary.

p50

B
Students color the painter's T-shirt red.
Students color the chef's hair brown.
Students color the nurse's clothes green.
Students color the zookeeper's cap blue.

C
1. zookeeper
2. chef
3. painter
4. nurse

p51

A
1. b
2. a
3. a

B
A
a. 2
b. 1
c. 3

pp52–53

A
a, b

B
1. people
2. houses
3. chef
4. zookeeper
5. animals

C
1. painter, d
2. zookeeper, c
3. chef, a
4. nurse, b

D
1. is she, She's
2. are they, They're
3. is he, He's
4. is she, She's

E
1. is she, She's a nurse.
2. are they, They're painters.
3. is he, He's a chef.
4. is she, She's a zookeeper.

p54

B
1. postal worker
2. barber
3. server
4. librarian

C
1. server
2. postal worker
3. librarian
4. barber

p55

A
A. 2
B. 3
C. 1

B
B
1. ×
2. ✓
3. ✓

pp56–57

A
1. Yes
2. No

B
1. a
2. b
3. b

C
1. b, postal worker
2. a, librarian
3. a, server
4. b, barber

D
1. librarian
2. postal worker
3. server
4. barber

E
1. Where
2. What
3. Where
4. What

pp58–59

A
A

B
1. ✓
2. ✓
3. ✓
4. ✓

C
1. ×
2. ✓
3. ✓
4. ×

D
1. b
2. c
3. b
4. a
5. b

E
(1) Barbers
(2) servers
(3) postal worker
(4) librarian

pp60–61

A
Underline: at, on, on

B
1. It's on Elm Street.
2. It is a big place.
3. It has a lot of rooms.

C
Answers will vary.

D
Answers will vary.

pp62–63

A
1. Answers will vary.
2. Answers will vary.

B
1. The clock shows the time in 148 cities around the world.
2. Answers will vary.

p64

B
Students color the sun orange.
Students color the second girl's shirt green.
Students color the third girl's pants blue.
Students color the fourth girl's shoes red.

C
1. walk to school
2. get dressed
3. wash my face
4. morning

p65

A
1. 9:00 a.m.
2. 6:00 a.m.
3. 5:00 p.m.

B
A
1. ×
2. ✓
3. ✓

pp66–67

A
a

B
1. on a video call
2. Hong Kong
3. 3:00 p.m.
4. has English class
5. walks to school

C
1. morning, b
2. wash my face, a
3. gets dressed, d
4. walk to school, c

D
1. 6:30 a.m.
2. 6:45 a.m.
3. 7:30 a.m.
4. 8:00 a.m.

E
1. gets up
2. washes his face
3. gets dressed
4. walks to school

p68

B
1. 10:00
2. 6:00
3. 2:00
4. Saturday July 6

C
1. days
2. afternoon
3. evening
4. sleep

p69

A
1. a
2. b
3. b

B
B
a. 3
b. 1
c. 2

pp70–71

A
1. No
2. Yes

B
1. a
2. b
3. b

C
1. b, afternoon
2. a, sleep
3. b, day
4. a, evening

D
eats lunch
has class
has a soccer game
walks home

E
1. First, she eats lunch.
2. Next, she has class.
3. Then, she has a soccer game.
4. Finally, she walks home.

pp72–73

A
A

B
1. ✓
2. ×
3. ✓
4. ×

C
1. ×
2. ✓
3. ✓
4. ×

D
1. b
2. a
3. c
4. b
5. a

E
(1) morning
(2) gets dressed
(3) washes his face
(4) walks to school

pp74–75

A
Underline: a.m., p.m., p.m., p.m.

B
Person: Doctor Park
Day: today
Time: 4:30 p.m.
Reason: feels sick

C
Answers will vary.

D
Answers will vary.

pp76–77

A
1. Answers will vary.
2. Answers will vary.

B
1. Chopsticks are 7,000 years old.
2. Answers will vary.

p78

B
Students color the chicken yellow.
Students color the cabbage green.
Students color the soup orange.
Students color the onion red.

C
1. onion
2. cabbage
3. soup
4. chicken

p79

A
1. water
2. book
3. picture

B
B
a. 2
b. 3
c. 1

pp80–81

A
a

B
1. soup
2. mom
3. doesn't have
4. onions
5. 20

C
1. soup, c
2. onions, a
3. cabbage, d
4. chicken, b

D
1. Amy has
2. Amy has
3. Amy doesn't have
4. Amy has

E
1. have
2. have
3. don't have
4. have

p82

B
1. sweetcorn
2. milk
3. sausages
4. potatoes

C
1. sausages
2. potato
3. sweetcorn
4. Milk

p83

A
1. ×
2. ✓
3. ✓

B
A
1. ×
2. ✓
3. ×

pp84–85

A
1. No
2. Yes

B
1. b
2. a
3. b

C
1. b, sweetcorn
2. b, milk
3. a, sausages
4. a, potatoes

D
wants: milk
doesn't want: potatoes, sausages, sweetcorn

E
1. doesn't want potatoes
2. doesn't want sausages
3. doesn't want sweetcorn
4. wants milk

pp86–87

A
B

B
1. ×
2. ✓
3. ×
4. ×

C
1. ×
2. ×
3. ×
4. ✓

D
1. b
2. a
3. b
4. a
5. c

E
(1) cabbage
(2) onions
(3) potatoes
(4) sweetcorn

pp88–89

A
Underline please, please, Thank you, Thank you

B
1. I want the chicken soup, please.
2. I do
3. Sure

C
Answers will vary.

D
Answers will vary.

Workbook Answer Key

pp91–92

A
A. 2
B. 3
C. 1

B
1. ×
2. ✓
3. ×

C
1. b
2. a
3. a
4. c

D
1. drawing, b
2. classmates, a
3. sticker, b
4. decorations, a

E
1. decorations
2. classmates
3. stickers
4. drawing

F
1. sticker
2. decorations
3. classmates
4. drawing

pp93–94

A
1. ×
2. ✓

B
1. ×
2. ✓
3. ✓

C
1. Yes
2. Yes
3. Yes
4. No
5. Yes
6. Yes

D
1. a
2. c
3. b

E
1. classroom
2. globe
3. coat hook
4. poster

Speak
Circle: Can, Can
Answers will vary.

pp95–96

A
A. 2
B. 1
C. 3

B
1. ✓
2. ×
3. ✓

C
1. b
2. b
3. c
4. a

D
1. run, a
2. jump, b
3. walk, a
4. swing, b

E
1. jump
2. walk
3. run
4. swing

F
1. swing
2. walk
3. jump
4. run

pp97–98

A
1. ×
2. ✓

B
1. ×
2. ✓
3. ×

C
1. Yes
2. No
3. Yes
4. No
5. No
6. Yes

D
1. b
2. a
3. a

E
1. rollerblade
2. hobby
3. sports
4. hop

Speak
Circle: every Wednesday, From Monday to Friday, on the weekend
Answers will vary.

pp99–100

A
1. ×
2. ✓

B
1. ×
2. ✓
3. ×

C
1. c
2. a
3. a
4. b

D
1. smartphone, b
2. vase, a
3. T-shirt, a
4. clothes, b

E
1. clothes
2. vase
3. T-shirt
4. smartphone

F
1. T-shirt
2. vase
3. clothes
4. smartphone

pp101–102

A
A. 3
B. 1
C. 2

B
1. ✓
2. ✓
3. ×

C
1. No
2. No
3. No
4. Yes
5. Yes
6. Yes

D
1. a

2. a
3. b

E
1. shopping carts
2. camera
3. toys
4. plane

Speak
Circle: What about you?
What is your favorite store?
Answers will vary.

pp103–104

A
1. ✓
2. ×

B
1. ✓
2. ✓
3. ×

C
1. a
2. b
3. c
4. a

D
1. nurse, b
2. zookeeper, a
3. painter, a
4. chef, b

E
1. chef
2. zookeeper
3. nurse
4. painter

F
1. painter
2. chef
3. zookeeper
4. nurse

pp105–106

A
A. 1
B. 3
C. 2

B
1. ×
2. ×
3. ✓

C
1. No
2. Yes
3. No
4. No
5. Yes
6. Yes

D
1. b
2. a
3. c

E
1. barber
2. postal worker
3. server
4. librarian

Speak
Circle: on Park street, at a small restaurant
Answers will vary.

pp107–108

A
1. ×
2. ✓

B
1. ✓
2. ×
3. ✓

C
1. a
2. b
3. c
4. a

D
1. wash my face, b
2. get dressed, a
3. walk to school, a
4. morning, b

E
1. get dressed
2. morning
3. wash my face
4. walk to school

F
1. walk to school
2. wash my face
3. morning
4. get dressed

pp109–110

A
A. 2
B. 3
C. 1

B
1. ✓
2. ×
3. ✓

C
1. No
2. Yes
3. Yes
4. No
5. Yes
6. Yes

D
1. a
2. c
3. b

E
1. sleep
2. afternoon
3. day
4. evening

Speak
Circle: 11:00 a.m. on Tuesday, 7:00 in the morning
Answers will vary.

pp111–112

A
1. ×
2. ✓

B
1. ×
2. ✓
3. ×

C
1. a
2. c
3. b
4. c

D
1. soup, a
2. onion, b
3. chicken, b
4. cabbage, a

E
1. cabbage
2. soup
3. onions
4. chicken

F
1. onion
2. cabbage
3. soup
4. chicken

pp113–114

A
A. 3
B. 2
C. 1

B
1. ×
2. ✓
3. ×

C
1. Yes
2. No
3. Yes
4. Yes
5. Yes
6. No

D
1. b
2. a
3. c

E
1. potato
2. milk
3. sweetcorn
4. sausages

Speak
Circle: please, Thank you
Answers will vary.

Audio Script

p7

B

Classrooms Around the World

These children go to school on a boat. Their classroom is on the river!

p8

A

classmates, decorations, drawing, sticker

B

The classmates are sitting in red chairs.
The decorations are blue.
The drawing is yellow.
The sticker is green.

C

1. decorations
2. sticker
3. classmates
4. drawing

p9

A

1. This is a drawing of my cat. Her name is Sally. She's orange.
2. Tom is my classmate. He's seven years old. He likes reading.
3. I'm at my new school. I have many classes today. First, we have math.

B

A Busy First Day

It's our first day of school and we're making a learning tree. The tree is what we're learning this year.
First, my classmates and I put the decorations on the tree. What are those, Ann?
Orange paper flowers. I love flowers.
Nice! Then, we draw things. What's that, Jon?
It's a dinosaur. It has stickers for teeth and eyes! What is that, Zoe?
This is a guitar. I want to learn music this year!

p10

B

See script of *A Busy First Day*.

C

1. They are my favorite classmates.
2. Those are our decorations.
3. We have a lot of stickers.
4. You can see my drawing on my desk.

p11

D

See script of *A Busy First Day*.

p12

A

classroom, coat hooks, globe, poster

B

1. There is a globe on the bookcase.
2. The poster is on the wall.
3. The teacher is in the classroom.
4. The coat hooks are in the hall.

C

1. They are making a poster for the wall.
2. My teacher has a globe on her desk.
3. Our classroom is very big.
4. My coat hook is next to the door.

p13

A

This is Matt's drawing of his math classroom. There is a book on the desk and a chair by the desk.
May is making a picture. She is using paper, glue, and scissors.
This is Paul's classroom. There are a lot of books on the bookcase.

B

Guess What?

It's the end of class. Now it's fun time! Let's play the game "What is it?". OK, it's big and round. It isn't a ball. What is it?
Is it a globe?
Yes, it is! Good! OK. What are these? They're small. They're for coats.
Are they coat hooks?
Yes, they are! Next. It's square. It's on the wall! What is this?
It's a poster! Yay!
Last one—you're in it now. What is this?
Is it a classroom?
Yes, it is! Very good!
Yay!

p14

B

See script of *Guess What?*.

C

1. Our drawings are on the wall in the classroom.
2. The coat hooks are near the door.
3. We can see a lot of countries on the globe.
4. There are planets on that poster.

p15

D

See script of *Guess What?*.

p16

A

Happy New Year

Amy and Lee are classmates. They make decorations for Lunar New Year. Lunar means *moon*.
What are those decorations, Lee?
They're paper lamps.
How do you make them?
First, get some paper. Then, cut some lines. Next, open the paper. Last, glue the paper together.
Wow! I like it! Is that your rabbit poster, Lee?
Yes, it is. It's the Year of the Rabbit!
Nice! What's the drawing?
It's a cake. I love New Year's cake! Yum!

p17

D

See script of *Happy New Year*.

E

See script of *Happy New Year*.

p18

A

Let's make decorations for the school party.
Good idea! I have some crayons, pencils, and stickers.
Can I have some crayons?
What colors do you want?
Can you give me the red and green crayons, please?
Sure. Here they are.

p21

B

Zorbing

Zorbing is a fun game. Children can do it, too. You go inside a big, round ball and move. You can go fast. You can walk on water, too!

p22

A
jump, run, swing, walk

B
The girl in the green shirt is jumping.
The boy in the red cap is swinging.
The boy in the blue shoes is running.
The girl in the yellow skirt is walking.

C
1. swing
2. jump
3. walk
4. run

p23

A
1. Kim plays soccer with her friends. Kim runs with the ball.
2. Pedro doesn't take the bus to school. Pedro walks to school with his friends.
3. Sue likes sports. Sue swims in a pool. Sue jumps into the water with her sister.

B
A Time for Sports
Beth and Adam can go back in time.
Where are we?
We're in Greece 2,000 years back in time. Walk over here.
Can you see those people?
What are they doing?
They are playing games. It's the first Olympics.
Look at those men run!
They can run fast.
Can they jump, too?
That man can jump very high!
He can swing, too. Look!
He's swinging on a rope!
Can you swing on the rope, Beth?
No, I can't. It's too high! But I can go back in time! Let's go home now.

p24

B
See script of *A Time for Sports*.

C
1. They walk to school.
2. She runs in the park.
3. Don't jump in class!
4. Ceci can swing high.

p25

D
See script of *A Time for Sports*.

p26

A
hobby, hop, rollerblade, sports

B
1. Maria and Alba's hobby is dancing.
2. Ben plays sports in the park.
3. Cara likes to rollerblade in the park.
4. Harry hops on one foot for hopscotch.

C
1. My brother and I can hop fast.
2. We rollerblade at the park on Saturday.
3. I have a fun hobby.
4. We play many sports at school.

p27

A
Dan can swim. Dan's hobby is swimming. Dan swims on Tuesday with his friends.
Saturdays are fun at the park! You can ride your bike. You can play games
Sue likes sports. Sue plays sports at school. Sue plays sports after school, too.

B
A Fun Hobby
I'm Jade. I like to rollerblade. It's my hobby. I can rollerblade in many ways. I can hop. I can jump. I like to go very fast. I don't like to go slow. I don't like to walk. I rollerblade to many places. I rollerblade to the park. I rollerblade in races. I rollerblade to school. It's a fast way to go to school. I rollerblade every day. Why do I rollerblade? It's good for me. It's fun, too!

p28

B
See script of *A Fun Hobby*.

C
1. I rollerblade in the park with my friends.
2. We play hopscotch at school. I can hop really high.
3. I do my hobby on the weekend. I like to climb. It's fun!
4. I like to play a lot of sports.

p29

D
See script of *A Fun Hobby*.

p30

A
A New Sport
Luke plays sports at school. He plays soccer on Tuesday and tennis on Friday. Now he wants to try a new sport. He talks to his friend, Tony.
Let's try a new sport, Tony.
OK! What can you do?
I run fast. I jump high.
Hmm. Do you like basketball?
No, I don't.
Hey, Jade! We want to try a new sport. What can you do?
Well, I can rollerblade fast!
Let's try to rollerblade!
OK! Let's do it!

p31

D
See script of *A New Sport*.

E
See script of *A New Sport*.

p32

A
My Weekly Routine
by Jane
I do karate every Monday. From Wednesday to Friday, I run in the mornings. But I don't play sports on the weekend. I walk in the park with my friends. And I ride my bike. I sleep a lot, too.

p35

B
Covent Garden
This market is in London, England. You can buy flowers from around the world. A lot of people go there. It's fun!

p36

A
clothes, smartphone, T-shirt, vase

B
The girl is talking to her friend on her purple smartphone.
There is an orange vase in the store.
The sales clerk has a blue T-shirt.
The boy is looking at some green clothes.

C
1. clothes
2. smartphone
3. vase
4. T-shirt

p37

A
1. Ted is at the store. He buys some clothes. The T-shirt is 20 dollars.
2. Sue is at the mall with her mom. Sue's mom wants to buy a vase. The vase is 10 dollars.
3. Ann is at the store. Ann wants to buy stickers. The stickers are 90 cents.

B

A Gift for Mom

Tara is at a market with her father. She talks to the sales clerk.
I want to buy a gift for my mom.
We have clothes.
Mom likes clothes! Look at her picture on my smartphone. She has red hair like me.
She's pretty. Well, we have red T-shirts.
Mom doesn't like T-shirts. She has nice shirts.
What about a vase? This is 15 dollars.
Oh, she doesn't have a vase! But I don't have 15 dollars.
I have a small vase for eight dollars.
Great! I have 10 dollars. I can buy this vase.

p38

B

See script of *A Gift for Mom.*

C

1. My mom likes clothes.
2. This is my new smartphone.
3. My mom doesn't like T-shirts.
4. There are vases in the market.

p39

D

See script of *A Gift for Mom.*

p40

A

camera, plane, shopping cart, toy

B

1. Jim looks at the toy robots in the store.
2. I have a red camera. Look!
3. The toy planes are only five dollars today. Wow!
4. There is a scooter. It's in the shopping cart.

C

1. There are a lot of toys in the store.
2. That shopping cart is dirty.
3. My brother's camera is black.
4. Tom has a small plane.

p41

A

1. They close the toy store in the mall on Sunday.
2. My birthday is soon. It's on Friday!
3. It's Wednesday. I have an art class today.

B

Megamarket

Welcome to Megamarket! Today is Monday. We have cameras for 40 dollars. They're in the camera store. On Tuesday, we have planes for five dollars in the toy store. On Friday, paint is 99 cents. It's in the art store. Saturday is a big shopping day! You can eat ice cream for 25 cents! It's in the ice cream store. Shopping carts are at the front of the store.
Don't stay home this week. Shop at Megamarket!

p42

B

See script of *Megamarket.*

C

1. There are a lot of planes at the store. Carl likes planes. He buys a new one.
2. We put our things in the shopping cart at the store.
3. Mia and her mom are at the store. Mia sees a fun toy.
4. Ben likes the red camera. It's 50 dollars. He wants to buy it.

p43

D

See script of *Megamarket.*

p44

A

The Grand Bazaar

by Ian Smith

The Grand Bazaar is in Turkey. It's an old market with a lot of stores. I go with my friend, Ata. Ata knows all the places! We go on Saturday. It's our friend's birthday on Sunday. We want to buy a birthday gift for our friend here. I like toys. Ata likes clothes. Ata buys a T- shirt. It's five dollars. I buy some candy. It's 50 cents! Now, what can we buy for our friend? It's fun to go shopping at the Grand Bazaar!

p45

D

See script of *The Grand Bazaar.*

E

See script of *The Grand Bazaar.*

p46

A

What's your favorite store?
It's the toy store. I can buy scooters there.
Nice!
What about you? What's your favorite store?
I like the clothes store. I can buy T-shirts there.

p49

B

A Wildlife Photographer

This man is a wildlife photographer. He takes photos of animals. He travels all around the world to take photos. He takes photos in hot places and in cold places. It's a fun job.

p50

A

chef, nurse, painter, zookeeper

B

The painter's T-shirt is red.
The chef's hair is brown.
The nurse is wearing green clothes.
The zookeeper has a blue cap.

C

1. zookeeper
2. chef
3. painter
4. nurse

p51

A

1. This is my house. It's small. I live here with my family.
2. I'm in Rome. It's a very old city. There are many old buildings here.
3. I'm from Ghana. It's a country in Africa.

B

Working Around the World

Hi! I'm Tam. I'm talking to people around the world. Where do they work? What do they do? This is Mary and Bill from Scotland. Mary's a nurse. Bill's a painter.
Hello, I'm Mary. I help sick people.
I'm Bill. I paint houses with my son, Tom.
And this is Raúl in Mexico. Who is he? Hello, Raúl.
Hello, Tam. I'm a chef. I work in a restaurant.
And last, this is Meg.
What do you do, Meg?
I'm a zookeeper. I work with animals at a zoo.
Thanks everybody!

p52

B

See script of *Working Around the World.*

C

This is my mom. She's a painter.
My uncle is a zookeeper. I go see him at work.
This is my dad. He's a chef.

Aunt Emma is a nurse. She's nice.

p53

D

See script of *Working Around the World*.

p54

A

barber, librarian, postal worker, server

B

1. The postal worker has a lot of mail today.
2. The barber cuts the boy's hair.
3. The server gives the woman her tea.
4. The librarian helps people find books.

C

1. My sister is a server.
2. The postal worker is in the van.
3. The librarian is at her desk.
4. My dad is a barber in the city.

p55

A

1. Susan lives in Leeds. Her house is at 34 Main Street.
2. Ming goes to see his grandparents at 22 Kings Road.
3. The toy store is at 18 North Road. Let's go!

B

New Friends

Han lives in a new city. He asks Lee about his new friends.

Lee, where does Zoe work?

Zoe's a librarian.

Where is the library?

The library is at 22 Oak Street.

OK. And what does Jack do?

Jack is a postal worker. He works at the post office.

And Brian? Where does Brian work?

He works at Maple Restaurant. He's a server.

Where is Maple Restaurant?

It's at 65 Elm Street.

What does Mr. Kim do?

He's a barber.

Where is his shop?

It's not far. I can show you!

Let's go!

p56

B

See script of *New Friends*.

C

1. A postal worker works in a post office.
2. A librarian works in a library.
3. A server works in a restaurant.
4. A barber works in a barbershop.

p57

D

See script of *New Friends*.

p58

A

The Guessing Game

Ellie and Max play a game at home.

Ready? Let's play! They work at 24 Park Street. Who are they?

Hmm. Barbers?

No. They work in a restaurant.

Are they servers?

Yes! Your turn.

OK. This person lives at 45 Main Street.

Hmm. I know that address. That's your house!

What does this person do?

Is it your mom? She's a postal worker!

No! My dad's a postal worker! My mom's a librarian.

You win!

p59

D

See script of *The Guessing Game*.

E

See script of *The Guessing Game*.

p60

A

The City Hospital

My mom is a nurse. She works at a hospital. The hospital is on Elm Street. It is a big place, and it has a lot of rooms. My mom works on the top floor of the building. She helps sick people.

p63

B

What's the Time?

This is the World Clock. It's a big clock. The clock shows the time in 148 cities around the world.

p64

A

get dressed, morning, walk to school, wash my face

B

The sun in the morning is orange.

The girl in the green shirt washes her face.

The girl gets dressed in blue pants.

The girl walks to school in her red shoes.

C

1. walk to school
2. get dressed
3. wash my face
4. morning

p65

A

1. Kristi has three classes today. First, she has math at 9:00 a.m.
2. Paul gets up at 6:00 a.m. He eats breakfast. Then, he brushes his teeth.
3. First, Max does his homework. Then, he eats dinner at 5:00 p.m.

B

It's Early!

Yen is in England. Li is in Hong Kong. They're cousins. Li video calls Yen.

Good morning, Yen

It's early, Li!

It's 3:00 p.m.! I have English class at 3:30!

Well, it's 7:00 in the morning in England!

Oh, sorry! What time do you get up?

I get up at 6:30 a.m. I wash my face at 6:45 and I get dressed at 7:30.

When do you walk to school?

At 8:00 a.m.

Now you can talk to me before school!

p66

B

See script of *It's Early!*.

C

1. It's morning. It's time for breakfast.
2. I wash my face at 6:30 in the morning.
3. She gets dressed. Then she goes to school.
4. The boys walk to school at 8:00 a.m.

p67

D

See script of *It's Early!*.

p68

A

afternoon, day, evening, sleep

B

1. Ben goes to sleep at 10:00 p.m.
2. Ben has a party at six in the evening.
3. Ben has a soccer game in the afternoon.
4. Today is my favorite day. It's my birthday!

C

1. Tim walks to school on

sunny days.
2. Liz watches TV in the afternoon.
3. Yoko does homework in the evening.
4. Kim goes to sleep late on Saturday.

p69

A
1. It's morning. Tim drinks water. Then he eats breakfast.
2. Todd has a busy day. First, he goes to the market. Next, he does his homework.
3. In the afternoon, Sue watches TV. Then, she talks with her friends on the computer.

B
A Great Day
It's Friday afternoon. On most Fridays, Pam eats lunch first. Next, she has class.
Then, she has a soccer game. Finally, she walks home.
This Friday is different. Pam is on a school trip at the zoo. She learns about the animals. It's a fun day at the zoo.
Pam goes home in the evening and tells her mom about the zoo. They eat and watch TV.
Then, she goes to sleep.
What a great day!

p70

B
See script of *A Great Day*.

C
1. I do my homework in the afternoon.
2. I go to bed at 8:00 p.m. I go to sleep at 8:30 p.m.
3. It's a nice day today. It's sunny!
4. It is cold in the evening. The sun is gone now.

p71

D
See script of *A Great Day*.

p72

A
It's Sunday!
The clock rings. It's 6:30 a.m. Jae is tired. He wants to sleep. It's a school day. What does Jae do in the morning? First, Jae gets up. Next, he gets dressed and washes his face. Then, he eats breakfast. "Hurry up, Jae! Don't be late," says Jae's mom. Jae walks to school at 8:00 a.m. He sees his friends at the park. Why aren't they at school? Oh, no! It's not a school day. It's Sunday!

p73

D
See script of *It's Sunday!*.

E
See script of *It's Sunday!*.

p74

A
A Doctor's Appointment
Hello? This is Doctor Park's office. Can I help you?
This is Eric Gilbert. I want to see the doctor. I feel sick. Can I make an appointment today?
There are two times open today, 10:00 a.m. or 4:30 p.m.
I can come at 4:30 p.m.
Great! See you at 4:30 p.m., Eric.
Thanks. Bye!

p77

B
Time to Eat!
Chopsticks are 7,000 years old. A lot of people around the world eat food with chopsticks.
Some chopsticks are made from trees. They can be long or short.

p78

A
cabbage, chicken, onion, soup

B
The chicken is yellow.
The cabbage near the girl is green.
The soup is orange.
The onion is red.

C
1. onion
2. cabbage
3. soup
4. chicken

p79

A
1. It's very hot. Can I have water, please?
2. Can you give me that book, please? It looks fun.
3. Who is that? Can you show me a picture, please?

B
Kids Tell You How
Amy and Jo have a radio show about cooking.
What are you cooking today, Amy?
It's my mom's chicken soup.
Do you have everything to make the soup?
I have chicken and rice. I have cabbage and onions.
My mom uses apples. I don't have apples.
Can you tell me how to make the soup?
First, get a pot of water. Cook the chicken and onions. Then, put in the cabbage. Finally, put in the rice. Cook the soup for 20 minutes.
Can I try it?
Sure.
Thanks! Yum!

p80

B
See script of *Kids Tell You How*.

C
1. I like my mom's soup on cold days.
2. There are red onions on the burger.
3. I don't like cabbage in my salad.
4. They eat chicken sandwiches for lunch.

p81

D
See script of *Kids Tell You How*.

p82

A
milk, potato, sausage, sweetcorn

B
1. Tran is eating sweetcorn soup.
2. Tom drinks milk.
3. Yoko likes the sausages.
4. Mary has potatoes for lunch.

C
1. My sister doesn't eat sausages.
2. I have a potato with my chicken.
3. Do you eat sweetcorn for lunch?
4. Milk can help you sleep at night.

p83

A
1. Let's try the tea, Ann. You can put in milk.
2. Let's go to Rico's for lunch. We can eat pizza!
3. Let's cook dinner. I can make a salad. You can make the soup.

B
Making Lunch
It's lunchtime. Beth makes lunch. Theo watches TV.
Let's make lunch, Theo.
I'm watching TV, Beth.
OK. Do you want potatoes?
No.
Do you want sausages?

No.
Do you want sweetcorn?
No. Let's watch TV, Beth.
Beth cooks the food and then eats.
Do you want milk, Theo?
Yes. Thanks. Hey! What are you eating?

p84

B
See script of *Making Lunch*.

C
1. He wants to eat sweetcorn.
2. I want to drink milk.
3. Let's cook the sausages.
4. Yum! I like potatoes.

p85

D
See script of *Making Lunch*.

p86

A
From the Farm
Jill goes on a trip. She visits her friend, Zoe.
Zoe is eight years old. She lives in a small town. Zoe's family has a farm. They grow food.
"We have cabbage. We have onions. We have potatoes. And we have sweetcorn," Zoe says.
"Can I try the sweetcorn?" Jill asks Zoe.
"Yes, you can," Zoe says. "Our corn is great! Let's eat!"
Zoe is very happy. She likes her farm.
Jill likes Zoe's farm, too.

p87

D
See script of *From the Farm*.

E
See script of *From the Farm*.

p88

A
Today's Specials
Can I take your order?
I want the chicken soup, please.
OK, great. Do you want anything else?
Yes, I do. Can I have water, please?
Sure. Thank you for your order.
Thank you.

p91

A
Friendly Faces
We're drawing classmates' faces today. I'm drawing Tom's face. This is how I draw it. First, I draw an oval. Then, I use a ruler to draw eight lines on the oval. What are these lines? The lines help me draw his face. I draw the nose in the middle. Then, I draw the eyes on top and the mouth below. Next, I draw Tom's hair. Last, I color my drawing. Is that Tom's face? Yes, it is!

C
See script of *Friendly Faces*.

p92

D
1. drawing
2. classmates
3. sticker
4. decorations

p93

A
School Visit
Ada is visiting her older brother Noah at school.
Is this your classroom, Noah?
Yes, it is.
Is that your desk?
Yes, it is. I sit next to the window.
What are those?
Oh, these are drawings of turtles. And this is a poster about turtles.
What's that?
It's Fred. He's a turtle!
Hello, Fred! I like turtles. Can I go to school with you, Noah?
No, Ada, you can't. You can go to school next year.

C
See script of *School Visit*.

p94

D
1. The coat hooks are by the classroom door.
2. There's a globe on the bookcase.
3. Sue is making a poster about her favorite books.

p95

A
Don't Sleep!
Turtle and Rabbit run a race today. Sheep and Cat watch.
Here comes Rabbit. Look at her go!
She can run fast!
Can she jump over Turtle?
Yes, she can!
Oh, no, Turtle can't run. He's walking! He's very slow.
Yes, he is. Can Rabbit win?
Yes, she can! Rabbit is fast.
Look! Rabbit is stopping.
What's she doing?
She's going to sleep!
Now Turtle can win!
Turtle walks over the finish line!
Hooray!

C
See script of *Don't Sleep!*.

p96

D
1. run
2. jump
3. walk
4. swing

p97

A
Bella Learns New Things
Jo is from Finland. She's 10 years old. Jo has a dog, Bella. Jo has a fun hobby. Jo teaches Bella new things. Bella can hop. Bella can catch a ball. Bella likes to dance. Bella can dance with Jo. Bella can jump over things. Can Bella jump over Jo? No, she can't. But Bella can learn! Bella is smart.

C
See script of *Bella Learns New Things*.

p98

D
1. Carlos can hop on one leg.
2. Lucy likes to rollerblade at the park.
3. You can play sports in the gym at school.

p99

A
Cool Clothes
Jill and Lucy are at the mall. They see an older girl. They want to wear clothes like hers.
There's Mei!
I like Mei's clothes.
Me, too.
She has a cool T-shirt!
Yes! She has a cool smart-phone, too. You can buy that T-shirt here.
How much is it?
It's 30 dollars!
Wow! I only have 20 dollars.
Now I'm sad.
Don't be sad.
Hi, girls! I like your T-shirts!
You look cool!
Thanks, Mei!

C
See script of *Cool Clothes*.

p100

D
1. smartphone
2. vase
3. T-shirt
4. clothes

p101

A
A Trip to Tokyo
Phil visits his friend Yuto in Tokyo. They go shopping on Saturday.

I want a gift for my brother. I go home on Monday.
Does your brother have a camera?
No, he doesn't. But I only have 40 dollars.
You can buy a toy here. Does he have a plane?
No, he doesn't. But my brother likes planes.
Let's put it in the shopping cart.
Now, let's look for some clothes!

C
See script of *A Trip to Tokyo*.

p102

D
1. Tom buys a toy. It's a train.
2. Kim has a new camera.
3. We put the clothes in the shopping cart.

p103

A
My Favorite Job
May and Li do a school project about jobs.
Let's choose a job for our project, Li. Look at this picture.
Who are they?
They're chefs. They work in a restaurant.
Do you like cooking, May?
Yes!
Hmm. I don't! It's hot in the kitchen. Look at this picture.
Who's she?
She's a zookeeper. She works at a zoo in New York City.
That's a fun job! I like animals.
Me too! Let's do a project about zookeepers.
OK!

C
See script of *My Favorite Job*.

p104

D
1. nurse
2. zookeeper
3. painter
4. chef

p105

A
The Wrong Address
Eli is a postal worker. He takes a box to Mrs. Chen at the library. She's the librarian.
I have a box for you, Mrs. Chen.
Thank you! Umm, Eli?
Yes, Mrs. Chen?
This isn't my box!
Is this 455 Park Street?
No, it's 455 Mark Street. 455 Park Street is the barber's shop. This is for Mr. Lee, the barber.
Oh, no!
Don't worry. I can take it to Mr. Lee. He's my brother.
Oh, thank you!

C
See script of *The Wrong Address*.

p106

D
1. The librarian helps Tom find a book on the bookshelf.
2. The server puts the food on the tables.
3. The postal worker has a lot of mail in his bag today.

p107

A
Time for School
I'm Ali. I walk to school. It takes a long time. I get up at 6:00 a.m. and wash my face. It's early in the morning. Then I get dressed and eat breakfast. I walk to school at 8:00 a.m. with my friends. We cross water. We see a lot of animals. It's fun! I get to school at 8:30 a.m. Do you walk to school in the morning?

C
See script of *Time for School*.

p108

D
1. wash my face
2. get dressed
3. walk to school
4. morning

p109

A
It's Bedtime!
What does Jill do in the evening?
First, she watches TV. Then, she reads books. "It's bedtime!" says Jill's dad. But Jill doesn't stop reading. She reads at 9:00 p.m. She reads at 10:00 p.m. The next day Jill is sleepy at school. Jill goes home in the afternoon. "Let's play a game," says Jill's dad. Jill can't play a game. She wants more sleep. That night, Jill doesn't watch TV. She doesn't read books. She goes to sleep at 7:00 p.m.!

C
See script of *It's Bedtime!*.

p110

D
1. Tom eats a sandwich in the afternoon.
2. Emily reads with her mom in the evening.
3. Sam goes to sleep at 8:00 p.m.

p111

A
Onion Day
Mia likes food. She has a show about food.
Hello, I'm Mia. I'm at a market. It's Onion Day! Let's talk to a chef here. Can I try this onion soup, Chef?
Yes, you can! Do you like cabbage? There's cabbage in the soup. And there's chicken.
Yes, I like cabbage. I like chicken, too.
Try the soup.
Yum! This onion soup is great! Mm.
Thanks! Do you want to try onion candy?
Onion candy? I don't know...

C
See script of *Onion Day*.

p112

D
1. soup
2. onion
3. chicken
4. cabbage

p113

A
New Food
Lee's friend Onur is from Turkey. Lee and Onur have lunch at Onur's house. "Let's eat," says Onur. Lee sits at the table. There's a lot of food. There are potatoes. There's sweetcorn. There's chicken. There are sausages. "Let's eat the sausages," says Onur. Lee takes a big bite. His face is red. His eyes are big. "Quick! Drink this water!" says Onur. "It's hot!" says Lee. Onur laughs. "Yes, it's very hot!" "I like Turkish food!" says Lee.

C
See script of *New Food*.

p114

D
1. Ruby wants to drink milk.
2. Anna eats potatoes for lunch.
3. Bill likes sausages on his pizza.